Cyberbride

The Complete Online Guide to Planning Your Wedding

VERSION 1.0

By Denise & Alan Fields

Authors of the best-selling Bridal Bargains

COPYRIGHT PAGE AND ZESTY LO-CAL RECIPES

Congas, cuica, stand-up bass and tambourine by Denise Fields
Flugelhorn, bassoon, steel guitar and drums by Alan Fields
Cover, interior design and guitars by Epic Design
Index and additional keyboards by Doug Easton, New West Index
Catering for this book was provided by the Salt Lick
Backing vocals on "(She's got) Clicks and Bricks " by Ric Ocasek
Keyboard solo on "Dot-Com Blues" by Randy Newman
Additional harmony vocals on "Netscape #5" by John Hiatt

Special Thanks to PGW, especially Mark, Heather, Olu and Laurel.
Extra Special Thanks to Kirsten Bock, our invaluable helper.

Denise Fields appears courtesy of Helen and Max Coopwood.
Alan Fields appears courtesy of Patti and Howard Fields.

This book was written to the music of the Barenaked Ladies,
which probably explains a lot.

Distributed to the book trade by Publisher's Group West,
Berkeley, CA 1-800-788-3123. Printed in Canada.

Updates to this book are posted at www.CyberBrideBook.com. To order
this book, call 1-800-888-0385 or order online at www. windsorpeak.
com. Or send $11.95 plus $3 shipping to Windsor Peak Press, 436 Pine
Street, Boulder, Colorado 80302. Quantity discounts are available.

Questions or comments on this book? Contact the authors at (303) 442-
8792. Or fax them a note at (303) 442-3744. Or e-mail the authors at
questions@CyberBrideBook.com. Or write to them at the above address.

Library of Congress Cataloging-in-Publication Data
Fields, Denise
Fields, Alan
        CyberBrideBook: The Complete Online Guide to Planning your
Wedding (2nd edition)/Denise and Alan Fields
        Includes index.
        1. Weddings—United States—Planning. 2. Consumer education—
United States. 3. Shopping—United States.
93-93751 LIC   ISBN 1-889392-06-5

Version 1.0

OVERVIEW

TABLE OF CONTENTS

Chapter 4
Create: Whip up a personal wedding web page in seconds

Chapter 5
Find: Need a DJ? Photographer?
Use the 'net to find local merchants

Icons

How It Works

Reality Check

Wish List

The Big Seven

Red Flags

Best of the Web

Tips and Tricks

For Better or Worse

Intro:

Get wired.

Get married.

A brief intro

to 'net

nuptials.

Imagine you are invited to a wedding in June 2012.

As you survey the crowd of invited guests, you note the out-of-town guests look particularly splendid today. Of course, they are all holograms—this wedding (like all nuptials this year) is being broadcast live on the Internet to out-of-town family members who couldn't make the trip. They are sitting in front of a camera at home, which beams their image to the pews in the church.

The crowd turns to see the bride entering the sanctuary. She looks radiant in her custom-made gown. Two months ago, the bride stepped inside a "virtual measurement center" that scanned her every curve and beamed those dimensions to a Hong Kong dress maker. The entire gown was designed and fitted online and was shipped overnight to the bride last week—at half the price of what wedding dresses used to cost.

Now the bridesmaids enter, carrying flowers that were picked yesterday in California, Hawaii and South America. They were arranged and shipped overnight to the church direct from the growers.

All the while, the "memory preservation company" (what photographers and videographers are now called) captures the whole scene on a digital camera. Gone are the days of separate still and video camera people. Now weddings are captured on tiny cameras that do both still and full motion video; a fully edited DVD is handed to the couple at the end of the reception with all the day's events.

Finally, at the reception, don't look for the gift table because it was phased out in 2005. Guests now hand the bride and groom a "gift e-card," which looks like a credit card. One swipe of this card at the couple's home computer reveals the gift purchased and a few simple buttons are pushed to arrange delivery after the honeymoon. Don't like the gift? Any gift can be instantly swapped for something more appropriate or returned for cash.

Sounds nuts, eh?

Well, our attempts at seeing the future of weddings might seem outlandish, but many of those technologies are brewing in research labs as we speak. And if that sounds crazy, consider trying to explain today's "wired" weddings to a bride from say, 1985. You'd have to explain:

❖ Telephones today aren't just cordless, but wireless. When you are stuck in traffic and running late to an appointment with your caterer, you just whip out your mobile phone and call ahead.

❖ Your entire bridal registry is "online." Don't like what gifts you registered for? Today you can go online, see what's been purchased and swap items on your registry—at 2am in your pajamas from your living room.

❖ Need to confer with your maid of honor across the country? Simply send her an "electronic mail" (e-mail, for short) that takes just seconds to deliver and costs a fraction of a first class stamp.

So, perhaps the previous page wasn't so outlandish, eh? The simple fact is this Internet thing has transformed weddings—with more big changes to come. But before you get caught up in "dot-com mania," you have to stop and ask yourself: what can the 'net do for brides and grooms today, right now? Where do you go online to do all this cool stuff? And what's more hype than reality at this point?

That's where we come in. As consumer advocates, we've made our career out of chronicling the ups and downs of the wedding industry. Our mission in a nutshell: make sense of all this 'net stuff for you.

First some background on us.

EVERYONE LOVES THE PILOT, EXCEPT THE CREW

As your cyberguides, let us introduce ourselves. We got into this crazy wedding book business way back in 1988, in the ancient pre-Internet days. We were planning our own wedding at the time and feeling a bit overwhelmed. Add to that some "post-college unemployment" (that is, we couldn't find any other job) and you've got all the ingredients for a new book publishing company.

Our first effort was *Austin Weddings*, a local guide to nuptials in the capital city. That led to editions for other Southwest cities and eventually to our first national effort: *Bridal Bargains* in 1990. That book was a big success, in no small

Real Wedding Tip

JARGON CHECK

We'll try to hold all the 'net jargon to a minimum in this book, but here are a few terms we couldn't resist using:

❖ **Snail Mail.** *Sending a letter via the US Postal system. The speed of a snail sums up how this compares to email.*

❖ **FAQ.** *As in "frequently asked questions," these are archives on the Internet that answer common queries.*

❖ **Hyperlink.** *The nifty part of the web that lets you click on an underlined word and be zapped to another (related) site instantly.*

❖ **Spam.** *Unwanted or unsolicited email pitches. Folks who send spam are "spammers."*

❖ **Portal.** *A big web site that aims to be entry point for your web surfing.*

part thanks to Oprah Winfrey. She recommended the book to her viewers in 1991 and ever since then we have be able to call ourselves "full-time consumer advocates and authors." (You can read about our other books at the back of this book).

While we have always included Internet stuff in our *Bridal Bargains* book, we quickly realized the "wedding web" was growing much faster than the space we had in that book to cover it. And the web was morphing from a money-savings bargain bazaar into a more general purpose wedding planning tool—hence we decided to dedicate an entire book to this subject, namely the book you are holding in your hands now.

We also have direct experience in launching a web site: our own site, BridalGown.com, launched in late 1999. This site incorporates the advice and tips we previously included in our book *Bridal Gown Guide* (now online for free) as well as designer reviews, online gown quotes and more.

And we have always viewed the web as a big part of our efforts to stay in touch with our readers. We included our email address in our books way back in 1995 and launched a general web site at WindsorPeak.com to provide free updates to our readers. You can read updates and news on this book at www.CyberBrideBook.com.

Look ma, no ads!

We have always been proud of our no-commercial policy. We don't take ads, commissions, fees or any other compensation from the companies we review and rate. We believe this insures our objectivity. The publisher, Windsor Peak Press, derives its sole income from the sale of books and other digital content connected to these books. Of course, the opinions expressed in this book are those of the authors.

The closest exit may be behind you

Discussing the Internet is a bit like nailing Jell-O to a wall. No matter how well you think you have a handle on this thing, it morphs into something new within a few days. Or hours.

So, in order to keep things fresh, visit our web site at CyberBrideBook.com. We'll try to keep you up to date on all the goings on with 'net nuptials.

How free is free?

Many wedding web sites are free for all to use; the only thing they ask is for you to "register." And that's the rub: how much should you give up in terms of privacy to access these web sites?

In a perfect world, you should be able to use all web sites for free. All the advice should be available to all, right?

Well, in the real world, most web sites are out to make a profit—and that means making revenue somehow. Some sites gather info on users to re-sell to telemarketers; others might just use it to pitch you on the site's own products or services.

And the authors of this book aren't immune: we collect user names, addresses, phone number and wedding dates on our site BridalGown.com. Why? We do this to track users to determine whether our marketing efforts are successful. We also offer a service on our site called BridalQuote, where we send off discount dress quote requests on behalf of our readers to reputable gown sellers. When users request a quote, their contact info is passed along to these discounters. This way users don't have to retype their info again and again.

Our feeling on this: as long as a site discloses what they are doing with your info and you agree to it, it's fine. These "privacy policies" are usually buried in the fine digital print of most web sites—read them carefully. If a site doesn't say what it will do with your personal info, then don't give it up.

We try to address this issue in this book with a "Red Flag" icon (see the icons page at the beginning of this book). When we discover a site that we believe overly invades your privacy, we'll try to flag it. Here are a couple of other tips:

❖ **Set up a separate email box for your wedding-related surfing.** Separate your personal or work email from your wedding correspondence by setting up a different email box with a site like Hotmail.com. Another bonus: this also protects your main email account from spam. (unwanted email pitches).

❖ **Be wary of contests or surveys.** Most are thinly veiled attempts to get your personal info to send spam.

The Big 7:

Sizing up the big seven wedding web sites.

We call 'em the Big Seven: the largest wedding "mega-sites." Unlike other sites that are dedicated to one part of the bridal process, web portals like "The Knot" and the "Wedding Channel" are the Wal-Marts of the online wedding world. They try to do and sell a little of everything.

A brief note on how we handle the Big Seven. This chapter will give you a general overview of each site, including what we think is most cool about each site (and what needs improvement). Later chapters will have a *section* called "The Big 7" that goes into more detail. Here we'll examine what these sites specifically offer on topics ranging from shopping to community, registries to personal web pages. (The sites are listed in alphabetical order).

Here is how the Big Seven stack up:

BLISS

Web: www.blissezine.com
What it is: Web-based bridal magazine.
Background: One of the first wedding web sites, Bliss was launched by Cheryl and Steven Galvez in 1995. Their nuptials the year before inspired the site, which the couple envisioned as a planning guide to other couples.

What you see: A rather cluttered interface with lots of links. The main page includes a "Cover Story," "Announcements" (which focuses on one couple's engagement story and wedding plans), "Latest Articles" and "Features" (which spotlights the site's interactive budget planner, chat rooms and more). Along the left side of the page, you can access the site's Library, Community, Ask the Experts, Shopping and About Us sections. While the design is pleasing (a subtle blue background with purple and blue highlights), we couldn't get past the clutter—do you really need 100 links in itsy-bitsy type off your home page?

Commercial Plug-A-Thon: Thankfully, there are very few banner ads or commercial plugs on the site. Yes, the site is linked to the Wedding Network (for their gift registry) and BarnesandNoble.com (for their bookstores), but these are played in a low-key manner.

[Figure 1: Bliss' online magazine format emphasizes articles and advice.]

What's Cool: Despite the entry page nightmare, the rest of Bliss is blissfully easy to navigate. Want dress info? Click on the "Fashion" section in their library and you'll find "guides" (to veils, tips and advice), "articles" on various gown topics, related message forums and even related books from their bookstore. There are also additional links to other web resources.

In the Community section, you can post questions to "ask the expert" forums on wedding etiquette, flowers or even "dance" issues. Additional "topical forums" focus on a dozen more topics, including "beauty," "budgeting" and "ethnic weddings." Want regional advice? Additional forums focus on both domestic locations (broken down by state and even city) and international cities (23 countries at last count). Also in the community section: tips and advice from brides, wedding tales, and archives from polls the site has run.

Needs work: Despite being live since 1995, Bliss still feels like a work in progress. We noticed the "Shopping in Bliss" section was still under construction as we went to press. Are they kidding? Other wedding web sites long figured out how to sell things, so Bliss' absence in this hot category is puzzling. We couldn't access the regional forums on our last visit, which was frustrating. The chat rooms on this site also seemed a bit lonely on a couple of visits. And we thought Bliss could have integrated its gift registry more into the site. Instead, you just get a link to the Wedding Network.

Bottom line: Great articles, good forums but a cluttered entry page and lack of shopping make this site's appeal limited.

The Knot

Web: www.theknot.com
What it is: The Amazon.com of wedding web sites.
Background: Started by a scrappy group of NYU film students in 1996 as the wedding section on American On-Line (AOL keyword: knot), the Knot has grown aggressively into the largest wedding web site online.

The stats on the Knot are rather amazing: 1 million visitors each month, 35,000 brides and grooms registered (for free) each month, 10,000 products for sales in their gift registry and 11,000 gown pictures on the site.

[**Figure 2: The Knot's colorful entry page is focused and well-organized.**]

The Knot has come a long way from its beginnings on AOL as a wedding advice section. First, the site added "Bridal Search," a database of bridal gown pictures in 1997. The site also added interactive planning tools (see Figure 3 on page 13), a gift registry, personal wedding web pages and more.

But that's not all— The Knot sort of sees itself as the "Time Warner" of wedding sites: it wants to have its tentacles in all forms of media, both online and off. In 1998, the Knot inked a three-book deal with Broadway Books and published its first title, *The Knot's Complete Guide to Weddings in the Real World,* in early 1999. This was followed shortly there after by *The Ultimate Gown Guide* (see box on page 16 for more details) and a wedding planner that debuted in 2000. In the future, the Knot plans a public television series on wedding planning.

The Knot crowned its achievements by going public in late 1999, raising a $32 million war chest to expand its media empire. The company is backed by cable shopping channel QVC (which owns 36%), America On-Line (8%) and various venture capitalists.

What You See: Yes, it's cluttered, but at least it's colorful. The Knot's web page looks intimidating at first blush, but we found the underlying organization to be good. The site lists seven "channels" (taking a cue from AOL, their earlier backer) with such topics as engagement, fashion and beauty. In the middle of the page is a list of current features. Next to that is a series of quick jumps to the Knot's registry, gift store and wedding shop. Lower down the page you'll find quick links to the Knot's planning tools (more on this below) and personal wedding web pages. Buried at the bottom of the page is a link to the Knot's chat and message boards, as well as a search box.

Commercial Plug-A-Thon: The Knot is certainly the most commercial of all wedding web sites and it's no wonder: about 65% of the site's revenue is derived by advertising and sponsorships (the balance by their gift registry and bridal product sales).

Hence, you'll see many advertising plugs, some obvious and others not-so-obvious. Yep, there are the ever-present banner ads and pitches for the Knot's Wedding Shop (where they hawk cameras, wedding bubbles and other bridal accessories). Click on the "Ask Carley" feature that lists a Q & A with the site's editor and you'll get the "advice of the day"—plus a nice plug for Nutrisystems or a low-rate VISA card (both Knot "partners").

In the not-so-obvious category, the Knot doesn't always reveal that it charges vendors for "preferred" listing in their site. Check out the Wedding Photographers Network, which the Knot touts as a great way to find local photographers. Just pop in your area code, type of photography you want and a budget—then you get a list of photographers! Great, but the Knot "forgets" to mention that photographers pay $720 a year to come up at the top of the search list. Another example: honeymoon articles often feature a specific resort with a convenient link to that resort's home page. Nowhere does the Knot label these "articles" as advertisements (which they are, as the Knot gets paid from these sponsors).

The Knot defends these practices by saying they are a for-profit business (although they've lost $10 million dollars since their inception). And we realize the 'net often blurs the line between editorial and advertising. But as the country's largest wedding web site, the Knot should lead by example. And clearly labeling ads and paid-for plugs would be a step in the right direction.

What's cool: The Knot divides its content into four areas: tools, ideas, community and registry. Here's a brief overview of each feature:

1 Tools. This area contains the Knot's coolest features—an interactive wedding budget calculator, checklist, gown search, guest list manager and more. Here's a brief overview, in alphabetical order:

❖ **Gown Search:** This is a database of 15,000 gown pictures from 140 designers. What makes this feature powerful is their database: you can search for a gown by price, designer, silhouette and more—and then save the results to a list of gowns to view later. This tool also contains pictures of bridesmaids dresses, mothers gowns, and flower girl dresses.

❖ **Big Day Budgeter:** Create a personalized budget for each category of your wedding and reception. The Knot provides specific suggestions for what certain budgets can buy. You can save your budget information online and update it over time.

❖ **Local Vendor Finder:** Looking for a baker in Boston? A florist in Fargo? The Knot lists 13,000 vendors in 52 cities nationwide, in partnership with the Wedding Pages magazine (which the Knot bought in February 2000 for $8 million).

❖ **Personal Wedding Web Pages:** This area lets you create a three-page wedding web page that describes your wedding (ceremony details, lodging/travel info) as well as photos and personal stories from the couple. Of course, there is a link (plug) for the Knot's registry so guests can quickly jump to that section.

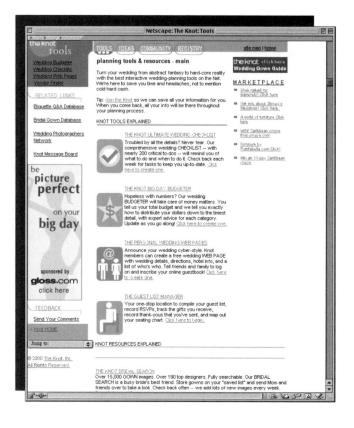

Figure 3: The Knot's planning tools section includes an online budgeter, checklist and guest list manager.

❖ **Wedding Checklist:** A week-by-week personalized to-do list based on your wedding date. The tool has daily to-do's and lets you check off completed items.

❖ **Wedding Guest List Manager:** Basically an online address book, this tool lets you track guest address info, total guests invited and guest responses. Cool feature: you can also create seating charts and record gifts received (and thank you's sent out—or see how far behind you are).

❖ **And that's not all.** The Knot also offers their Diamond Finder (which includes the ability to appraise a diamond), the Wedding Photographer Network, Accessory Search and more.

We'll review these tools in-depth in subsequent chapters of this book. Suffice it to say, the Knot's interactive tools offer an amazing array of services to brides and grooms—and each is free.

2 **Ideas.** This is the advice section of the Knot. Here you'll find articles on engagement (proposal ideas, choosing a ring), general planning (questions to ask wedding vendors), wedding ideas (including ethnic traditions and second wedding topics), and apparel (trends, advice). Additional areas of the site focus on beauty, grooms, bridesmaids, "newlywed nesting" (setting up a house, registry advice), and honeymoons. By the way, the Knot also offers to book honeymoons through the online travel agency Click Trips, a Knot subsidiary.

Yes, much of this content is similar to what you'd find in bridal magazines—brief articles long on breathless prose and short on actual advice. For example, "Gown Shopping: How to Find Your Gown for Less" gives just four measly tips, including the no-brainer "Shop Sample Sales." Omitted is any mention of online gown discounters and mail order discounters like Discount Bridal Service. That's not by accident, of course (see below for more).

3 Community. This is where the Knot started: hosting wedding chats and message boards on AOL. Of course, like everything the Knot does, there are just MORE of them, all accessible from the Knot's web site or AOL. The Knot's chat section boasts 45 weekly hosted chats around the clock. The Knot's numerous message boards include such topics as "Wedding Dress Resale Classifieds Board" and the vendor referral board, where you can find brides listing their favorite local vendors. The Knot's Community section also includes subscribable newsletters that provide site updates, special promotions, bridal registries and accessories.

4 Registry. The Knot has its own in-house bridal gift registry with 10,000 products from 500 brands. As you might guess, this area includes traditional items like china and household appliances, as well as more hip alternatives (outdoor gear, travel and even home mortgages). Guests can order items online or via phone or fax 24 hours a day.

We'll explore online registries in depth in Chapter 9. Suffice it to say, the Knot offers many cool features: you can monitor what's been purchased online, modify selections, pick a delivery date, and more. About half of the products the Knot supplies are supplied by QVC (their part owner); QVC also provides the shipping and fulfillment for the Knot's registry as well.

Needs Work. With all this free stuff, what's not to love about the Knot?

Well, plenty as it turns out. We've watched this company closely since it's humble beginnings on AOL. And some days we wonder what happened to Junior.

The Knot's whole schtick was to provide a hip, online alternative to those old crusty bridal magazines. Snazzy graphics and articles that appeal to Gen-X sensibilities (a "downtown voice" as they say in SOHO) made the Knot a favorite among brides and grooms. But somewhere along the way, we got the feeling the Knot sold out to the same demons in the wedding industry they claim to abhor.

We would guess the Knot's mission to be quirky ran

The Knot Stumbles with Gown Guide

Some day the Knot's flawed *Ultimate Wedding Gown Guide* ($19.95, in bookstores or online) may make a good case study for a college course entitled "Intro to Bad Web Marketing Practices."

The book features 1000 gown pictures from over 200 designers. The Knot touts the book as "not a bridal magazine and these are not ads. It's a tool." The web site promotes the book as having gown "prices and style numbers."

Yet our examination of the guide indicates the gown style numbers are bogus in some cases. We found four major manufacturers in the book that had incorrect or intentionally misleading style numbers—in the book, Pronovias gowns are listed as P-1, P-2 and so on. However, Pronovias identifies its gowns with women's names and five-digit numbers. The guide also contains incorrect style numbers for Galina, Bianchi and Paloma Blanca.

Knot spokesperson Jessica Kleiman said all the info for the gown guide was provided by designers and that the Knot did not independently verify style numbers. The fact that the Knot failed to do basic fact-checking for a $20 book is unacceptable.

Why would manufacturers supply bogus dress numbers to the Knot? In the battle over discounting, some gown designers have been coding their gown numbers on the 'net and elsewhere, trying to foil brides from shopping around. If you don't know the correct gown number you can't order it at a discount online or via mail order. Yet, incorrect style numbers also make it difficult to find the gown in a store, since most retailers do not have the translated codes.

The *Ultimate Wedding Gown Guide* also fails the truth test in another regard: the Knot promises the book will give gown prices. What they forget to mention is that the book only gives gown price RANGES. The gown defines prices as $600 to $800; $800 to $1500; $1500 to $3000 and $3000 and up. It doesn't help you much to learn a gown is priced somewhere between $1500 to $3000.

The general shopping advice in the book is also flawed. On page 30, the guide claims gowns are "custom-made" for each bride. Wrong again—gowns are only ordered in generic sizes. When a bridal retailer special orders a dress for a customer, a dress is cut in a specific size (but not to the bride's exact measurements). Only a few very expensive couture designers offer to custom make gowns for brides.

head long into their desire to make a profit—and venture capitalists' demand to start showing revenues. In a mad dash for cash, the Knot has seemed to throw its credibility under the bus.

Case in point: the Knot's flawed *Gown Guide* book (or magazine as the site calls it). Besides the mistakes and gaffes in the book (see the box on the previous page), the Knot has been shameless in how it promotes the title. First, the Knot slapped a ridiculous $50 retail price on the book but never sold it for that price. Instead, it is offered online at $30 and, later after a price cut, $20. Worse still, the Knot had pitchmen attend bridal shows claiming that the $20 price was a special discount price "for that day only!" Forget the fact that Barnes & Noble was selling it at the same time for $20.

And that's just the beginning. The Knot is "riddled with advertorials," said the Wall Street Journal in a recent critique. And many of these ads are simply not labeled as such. As mentioned above, the Wedding Photography Network charges photographers $720 a year for preferred placement on the Knot's site—but you won't see that disclosure on the site.

The Knot also omits any mention of online gown discounters and mail order houses—and that's a calculated move to keep bridal gown designers happy. The designers supply all of the pictures (for free) to the Knot's Bridal Search, a massive traffic draw.

We've also been puzzled with the Knot's registry strategy. Unlike other sites that have linked with major department stores, the Knot's hawks its own, in-house products (many from partner QVC). It seems to us many folks like the brand association of major department stores. And the Knot must actually warehouse, stock and ship all those items—a bigger risk to consumers (and the Knot) than when a well-known department store takes on that task. Whether the Knot succeeds or fails in the future will probably be based on their fateful decision to go it alone in the online registry race.

So, it's a mixed review for the Knot. You've got to love the free, powerful planning tools. And the chats and message boards are extensive. Yet, the Knot's ethical lapses make us wonder if they will be able to build credibility with consumers.

MODERN BRIDE

Web: www.modernbride.com

What it is: The online outpost for the bridal magazine.

Background: Like most traditional media companies, Modern Bride was late establishing its online presence, ceding the territory to upstarts like the Knot. Modern Bride has tried to make up for lost time in the past year, adding new shopping sections and alliances with the Wedding Network's gift registry.

What you see: Lots of text. For a site run by a glossy fashion magazine, Modern Bride's web site is certainly lacking visuals. Or a cohesive design. Instead, pop to the page and you are greeted with two columns of text. While nicely organized, it is so busy that you are left wondering which direction to go. Perhaps a brief "site tour" would make sense to introduce folks to their myriad of offerings. Later the site features rainbow colored links

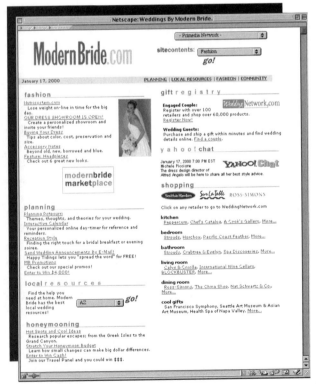

Figure 4 Pick a link, any link: Modern Bride's home page is loaded with options, but some aren't wedding-relevant.

that have a thrown-together-at-the-last-minute feel.

Commercial Plug-A-Thon: We couldn't decide what was more annoying, the banner ads or the entry page plug for Nutrisystems. Then there was a "pop-up" survey that arrived when we switched to the fashion section.

What's cool: Modern Bride's local resources section was the site's strong suit. Pick a region/state and you get a link to Modern Bride's local wedding magazine in that area. Select from 26 categories (from reception sites to bakeries, and more) and you get local resources—basically a list of prospects with their address, phone number, contact person and (in some cases) a link to that merchant's home page. We were impressed with the depth of these sites: a reception site search in one area turned up a massive list of possibilities. The only bummer: if you don't live in an area where Modern Bride has a "local edition" (17 major metro areas) you only get generic info.

Needs work: It's hard to pick just one area of this site that needs work—large parts of the site are a mess. Take the dress area—please! Sure, you can surf 60 designers' catalogs, add dresses to a personal "showroom" and compare dresses side by side. BUT, the site is so lacking in info it's comical: there are no dress prices (not even a rough range) or other info. Unlike sites that have their gown info arranged in a database (so you can search for certain gown features, styles or prices), Modern Bride just falls flat. That's a shocker from a magazine that makes its living selling gown ads—you'd think they'd have a better database than this.

The rest of the site similarly falls flat. The "interactive planning calendar" isn't much to look at—just a text listing of what to do at certain intervals. The chat area just leads you to a Yahoo message board. And the shopping section is merely a link to other sites and catalogs. Even the advice articles (check out the skimpy honeymoon section) seem half-baked.

Bottom line: Modern Bride's web site has a long way to go to catch up with their dot-com rivals—it has the feeling of a cobbled together effort that was ordered up by a publishing executive who thinks AOL is cutting edge. Without the strong local resources area, this site would have failed to make our top seven list.

Today's Bride

Web: www.todaysbride.com

What it is: The online version of the magazine by the same name.

What you see: Plenty of green. The site's three main planning tools (My Planner, My Registry, My Guests) are front and center, as is their bridal show locator. Along the side of the page are links for advice articles and a message board.

Commercial Plug A Thon: Besides a banner ad and plug for a vacation company, this site is rather devoid of ads and commercials.

What's Cool: The "Wedding Wisdom" section of this site is probably the highlight here: choose from 22 topics like "Perfect Honeymoons" and "Videography." The advice is good,

Figure 5: Today's Bride focuses on articles and advice.

but not great: the site warns of hidden charges with bridal gowns but then includes such squishy prose as "Your bridal gown is something you've dreamed about for a long time." On the upside: we liked the bridal show locator, which had 1400 events listed in a searchable database.

Needs Works: Overall, Today's Bride is probably the weakest of all the Big Seven. To see why, take a look at their "planning tools." Quite simply, they pale in comparison to the Wedding Channel or the Knot. The "My Planner" tool is a simple chart where you can record your budget and actual expenses. Yes, the site adds the totals, as well as provides you a space to write in details (like contact phone numbers for vendors). But that's it—there is no linked advice on saving money or the national averages for these categories. The site's gift registry is laughable as well—basically you enter all the items you are registered for (and which stores). Theoretically, your guests can then view the list and decide what to get you as a gift. But there are no live updates to show you what's been purchased (your guests are supposed to update your registry when they purchase a gift—yeah, right). Since Today's Bride doesn't have any registry partners, their registry lacks all the interactive features you can find on other sites. The Guest Manager is somewhat better: you can create reception table lists and record gifts and thank you's sent.

Bottom line: The advice articles on this site make it worth a brief visit, but you can skip their tools, which pale in comparison to other sites.

WEDDING BELLS

Web: www.weddingbells.com
What it is: The Great White North's biggest bridal magazine's slick web site, with versions for both the U.S. and Canada.
Background: Wedding Bells (the magazine) first debuted in Canada in 1985. The company made the transition to the internet in 1996 and the U.S. magazine market in 1999, launching a national magazine with six regional editions (Boston, Chicago, Dallas/Ft. Worth, San Francisco, and Southern California).

Figure 6: Wedding Bells boosts fancy graphics and smart advice.

What you see: A hybrid between the magazine world and the internet—large full color graphics and links. Don't worry: the inside pages omit the giant bride pictures, opting for a more traditional layout.

Commercial Plug A Thon: Yes, there are banner ads and plugs for their own wedding planner and "Wedding Ceremony Classics" CD, but most of the site is free from advertorials or other blatant commercials.

What's Cool: Although it's a bit hard to navigate around, the Wedding Bells site has some great content. They offer local vendor listings (in their six regional markets; see above for the list) as well as channels on fashion, ideas, planning/etiquette, travel, trends/traditions and a FAQ. Unlike other sites that offer useless advice or articles larded with advertorials, Wedding Bells advice section includes practical topics such as: "Entertaining Calculations" (how to figure out how many glasses a bottle of wine will yield, how many glasses to rent, etc), "Coming to Terms" (negotiating with vendors) and "The Last Word on Invitation Wording." Planning Priorities ask you a few basic questions about your wedding (formality, budget, etc) and then gives some advice on what to make a priority and what to skimp on. The extensive FAQ is very readable and packed with good info.

Needs Work: While the advice is great, other areas of the Wedding Bells site could use a boost. The Fashion channel features a measly 18 designers. Click on a designer and you get pictures of their gowns with a description (but no price info; and no online dealer locator). Yes, the graphics are high quality, but the lack of thumbnails makes this area hard to use. The site's local vendor finder is also limited in scope: we looked up bridal shops in Dallas and found just four listings. You have to scroll through several windows to access florists, DJ's and other wedding vendors. And while we liked the "high-style" graphics, the backgrounds got a bit annoying in some areas.

WEDDING CHANNEL

Web: www.weddingchannel.com
What it is: The #2 biggest wedding web site (behind the Knot.com).
Background: Launched in 1997, this site is the brainchild of Tim Gray and Raj Dhaka (both attorneys in previous lives). In 1999, The Wedding Channel landed two major partners: Bride's Magazine and Federated department stores. Bride's agreed to contribute content to the site and cross-promote the Wedding Channel in its pages. Federated Department stores bought 20% of the Wedding Channel and now offers its bridal registry online (for its Bloomingdales, Macy's, Bon March, Burdines, Goldsmiths, Lazarus and Rich's department stores).

What you see: A slickly designed home page with sections on Fashion, Shop & Register, What's New and links to chat areas, contests and various planning tools. While the site is pretty to look at, the organization is a bit confusing.

Commercial Plug-A-Thon: Each section of the The Wedding Channel features small ads for sponsors, although we didn't find the quantity of ads to be overwhelming. We did notice the Wedding Channel tends to bury content/articles below paid-for plugs. The "Travel" section is topped by pitches for honeymoons from Clicktrips.com (ironically, a Knot subsidiary) and Cruise411.com. Scroll down and you'll find actual articles on honeymoon destinations and planning. Once you get beyond the pitches, the advice is rather good (their article on Cabo San Lucas was detailed and well written).

What's cool: The Wedding Channel divides its content into six areas. Here's a brief overview:

- ❖ **Our Wedding.** You can create a personal wedding website with wedding logistics, out of town guest info, a gift registry, and more. This area also contains several cool tools: a customizable planning calendar, address book and guest manager.
- ❖ **Fashion & Beauty.** An online catalog of 8000 gowns, all searchable by designer, style or dress attribute (sleeveless, ball gown, etc.). This area also includes articles on health and beauty.
- ❖ **Shopping.** This area sells everything from wedding accessories to gifts for attendants.
- ❖ **Registry.** An online gift registry linked to Federated department stores; you can view what items have been purchased and change the registry at any time.
- ❖ **Planning.** This area contains advice articles on etiquette, planning, relationships and more. Also here: an interactive budget planner and a link to find local wedding vendors.
- ❖ **Travel.** Honeymoons, in a nutshell: deals, packages, articles and other related material.

And there's more. A section for "Grooms" includes advice on planning a rehearsal dinner, finding the right tux and buying a diamond. There's also a section for "Guests" on dress codes, gift ideas, etc. The site offers subscribable newsletters that give updates on the site, fashion, bride's stories and more.

What most impresses us about the Wedding Channel is the site's technology: check out the Fashion channels "sketchbook search" for wedding gowns. This powerful tool lets you search for dresses by one of 50 attributes (sleeve length, train style, waistline, etc). Wonder what a term means? Just roll your mouse over it and a simple black and white sketch appears in a picture box.

Figure 7: The Wedding Channel is attractive to look at, but much of the site is disorganized.

Needs work: Despite this site's fancy trappings, you can easily get lost in all this content. A reporter for the *Wall Street Journal* called the site "disorganized" and "hard to follow" and we have to agree—additional navigation bars and organization would be helpful. A site tour that would give new users an overview of all the content would also be an important improvement.

We were a bit puzzled with the site's local vendor search. When we searched for bridal retailers in our home town (Boulder, CO) we got 40 matches—including one for a shop in Los Angeles (a bit of a drive from here) and other listings for shops that had long since gone out of business.

Bottom Line: "Slick" doesn't always translate into "the most helpful" wedding web site—the Wedding Channel needs to make the site more user-friendly if they plan to overtake the

Knot. The interactive planning tools are rather amazing . . . but the advice articles could be vastly improved.

WedNet

Web: www.wednet.com

What it is: Lots of articles, advice and articles. Did we mention the articles?

Background: WedNet was launched in 1995 by Mark Williams, a Microsoft employee. The site launched "WedNet Store" to sell bridal accessories in 1998 and boasts about 90,000 visitors each month. (This site is NOT related to the Wedding Network, despite the similar name).

What you see: A busy site design with lots of text and links. "Elegant" is not the word we'd use to describe this site. Yes,

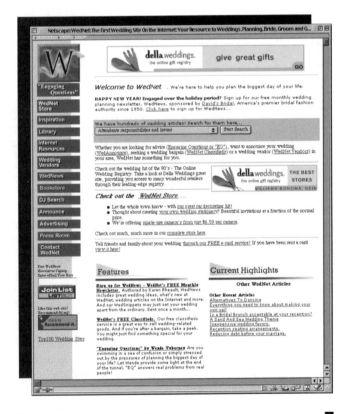

[Figure 8: Decent articles and a fully stocked bridal
store are WedNet's most useful features.]

the handy frame design gives you quick access to various features like the WedNet store and Library. But the site tries to cram too much into too little space.

Commercial Plug A Thon. This site has definitely sold its soul to the advertising gods. The entry page includes a prominent plug and ad for Della Weddings (an online registry reviewed later in this book). Then you'll notice the WedNews newsletter is sponsored by a bridal apparel chain. Subsequent pages have banner ads for various sponsors.

What's Cool: WedNet has a half dozen major content areas, including an online store and article archive. Here's an overview:

- ❖ **Engaging Questions:** This area dispenses the site's etiquette advice and includes topics both common (How should I include children in my wedding?) and more trivial (How can a bride keep from getting lipstick on the groom when they kiss at the end of the ceremony?). Most of the advice is good.
- ❖ **WedNet Store.** This online store sells everything from wedding cameras to books and videos. It's a bit chaotic to look at, but we were impressed with the breadth of offerings.
- ❖ **Wedding inspiration.** More articles, this time focused on consumer issues (questions to ask a video service, for example) and ideas (bridal shower themes). The advice is OK—one question they suggest you ask a videographer is "Are there any hidden costs?" Duh. If they were disclosed, then these costs wouldn't be hidden, eh?
- ❖ **Local vendor search**. This area asks you to select your state and then returns a huge list of wedding vendors and links to their home pages (when available).
- ❖ **DJ search.** Click here and you are taken to a DJ search from ProDJ.com.

Needs work. Even though this was one of the first wedding web sites, WedNet has been passed by on the technology side— unlike the Knot or Wedding Channel, you'll see no interactive planning or budget tools here. Instead, you get static articles (albeit a large number of them) which make for nice reading but not much else. The local vendor search engine is a good example of where WedNet needs to improve: instead of other sites that let you zero in on a metro area, you have to search by state. While that might work for Rhode Island, you can forget about California (there's such a massive, unorganized list of wedding vendors on the site we're not sure how anyone could make use of this). WedNet also has no chat areas or message boards.

Bottom line. This was a great site ... back in 1997. But times and technology have passed it by. Stop by for the articles or browse the shop, but don't expect much more.

Other sites

Bubbling under the Top Seven are several smaller sites. An interesting newcomer is **Ibride** (www.ibride.com, see Figure 9 below), which has a crisp and clean design. Check out the "Planning Your Wedding" section for local vendor listings and "Featured Topics" for message boards. Other parts of this site were still under construction when we last visited, but Ibride looks like it might develop into something interesting in the future.

Figure 9: Ibride.com is a good site to watch. The design is excellent even though much of the content is still under construction.

Martha Stewart has a special wedding section on her site (www.marthastewart.com/weddings/) and we're sure her fans will think this is a good thing. Various links take you to sections on flowers, favors, cakes, "for the bride" and more. Each section then gives you "a few of our favorite ideas" including a picture and description of an item (but no directions on how to make or buy it). Message boards and chat groups round out this site (although the topic areas are often too broad to be of much help to brides and grooms). Except for pitches for Martha's own stuff, this site is mostly free from advertising.

USABride.com has revamped their site now to include WedFind (to locate local vendors), a wedding store and plugs for online bridal registries (who are sponsors of the site). The wedding planning section includes a smattering of articles on 20-odd topics from catering to showers. Expect lots of blinking ads to pop up on this site.

Wedding Network (www.weddingnetwork.com) is affiliated with *Modern Bride* magazine. This site's big emphasis is their online gift registry (reviewed later in this book), but we also liked their planning tools (budgeter, task scheduler, event scheduler, guest manager). The gift registry boasts such stores as Bed Bath & Beyond, Smith & Hawken and Sur La Table. While this site occasionally hosts chats, it has no message boards or other community features. And watch out for all the sales pitches. In reviewing wedding web sites, the *Wall Street Journal* said of this site: "Crammed with thinly disguised advertorials and sweepstakes come-ons, this site is so promotional it makes the Knot look like *Consumer Reports*."

For better or worse

So, that's the Big 7; a motley group, eh? Certainly these sites are better than what was offered on the Internet for brides just a few years ago—and with time they will only get bigger (and hopefully) better. But let's get down to brass tacks: how can you really use the Internet to plan your wedding, track your budget and manager your guest list? We'll look at that in the next chapter.

Plan:

Track your bridal budget, appointments and guest list with these 'net planning tools.

Planning a weddings is a bit like mounting a small-scale military invasion. You've got to get 175 guests, 17 vendors, six bridesmaids, six groomsmen, two flower girls, and one ring bearer all to show up at exactly the right time and place. And, of course, all this must be done within a budget.

No wonder the business of planning this whole sha-bang has spawned all manner of books, videos, magazines and more. Heck, there are even people who make their living writing books on how to plan a wedding, as strange as THAT seems.

Into this fray, enter the Internet. Between you and your computer, there should be SOME way to harness the amazing power of the Internet to help manage this whole mess, right?

Well, the answer is a qualified "yes"—yes, you can use the Internet to help track your wedding budget, appointment calendar and even guest RSVP's and gifts. But, like everything out there in cyberspace, some tools are more helpful than others. We'll review which tools and sites have the most promise; and which ones are mostly hype.

First, here's a brief overview of how these "tools" work:

How It Works

Let's break down 'net planning tools into four general categories:

1 **Budget planners.** These tools can be as vague as a chart of "who pays for what" to powerful, interactive spreadsheets that help you track actual versus budgeted expenses. Many of the budget planners discussed in this chapter allow you to input your total budget and get back a chart of how much you should spend on each category, based on national average wedding costs.

2 **Interactive calendars.** These can merely be a "countdown" to your wedding (what you do when), or a periodic checklist telling you what to accomplish each week. The best sites will even email to "remind" you of certain tasks that should be accomplished at various intervals before your wedding.

3 **Guest list managers.** Just as they sound, these charts allow you to see all the guests you invite to which events, who has RSVP'd, what gifts you've received and what thank you notes you need to send.

4 **Software.** We found one site that lets you download free wedding planning software directly from their web site. Basically, this software does much of what the above tools accomplish, just offline as opposed to online.

Reality Check

Many of the whiz-bang interactive wedding planning tools on the Internet are fun to play around with . . . if (and this is a BIG if) you have a speedy Internet connection (see tip "Speed Demons" on the next page for specifics). And it would be helpful if you had access to the Internet at both home and work.

If you just have access to the 'net at work, you might find using online planning tools to be an exercise in frustration. That's because while it is neat to track guest responses and bridal appointments on the web, YOU still have to enter all this data by hand. Don't expect to do this all on a quick lunch break.

Another caveat: the budget tools online rely heavily on "national averages" to guide your spending. That's great for the big picture but not so good if you're looking for specific help for your situation. The tools are NOT scaled for those who live in big or small cities, nor do they take into account regional differences. After all a wedding in Iowa isn't going to be the same price as the same event in Southern California.

WISH LIST

Given the limitations of budget calculators, it's obvious what we'd put on our wish list. First, we'd like to see a budget calculator that divides wedding budgets into high, medium and low cost areas. And it should include some blunt advice—if you enter $5000 for a Manhattan wedding, the calculator should clearly indicate how unrealistic it is to try to plan a New York City wedding for that small an amount.

Another idea: How about a budget tool that allows you to choose either a "formal" wedding reception or something more "low key?" Right now, online budget planners and to-do checklists assume

SPEED DEMONS

Most folks access the 'net from home via "dial-up" connections. At work, you may have access to a speedy connection that moves at several times that pace, but your company may have restrictions on personal surfing.

Dial-up connections move data to and from the Internet at very pokey speeds (either 28K or 56K). Better alternatives are Digital Subscriber Lines (DSL) or cable modems, which range from 256K to 1500K. These connections have a major advantage (besides speed): they are "always on" and don't require you to dial in with each connection. On the downside, they can be pricey and are not available in all areas yet.

If you want to use the interactive wedding tools in this chapter, we'd recommend AT LEAST a DSL or cable modem connection. Trying to use an interactive budget planner with a 56K dial-up modem is like watching paint dry.

everyone is planning your "average wedding." But a formal wedding is much different than a garden ceremony followed by a home reception.

THE BIG SEVEN

The Big Seven web sites (see Ch. 2 for an overview of each) try to provide interactive planning tools to their users, with varying results. Here is an overview:

❖ **Modernbride.com** offers a couple planning tools that are marginally useful.

The first is a budget worksheet which allows you to enter a budget figure for various spending categories. Then as you buy things, you enter the actual cost of each category. The tool automatically totals up your spending and tracks any overages. While the concept is good, the execution could use some work. There are no instructions for how to use the worksheet, nor is their any explanation for their categories.

Modernbride's interactive calendar (www.modernbride.com /weddingplanning/calendar_frame.cfm) is only slightly better. Pop in your name, email address, age, city, state, zip, groom's name and email address (optional), then pick a wedding date. The result: a week by week checklist of things to do. When we popped in a wedding date that was only seven months ahead, the list said we ALREADY should have planned a reception, and picked out a bridal gown, among other items! Wow—talk about setting off a panic. Too bad the site doesn't offer any tips along with their checklist, like what to do if you don't have much time to plan or you have a limited budget.

❖ **Todaysbride.com.** Today's Bride (www.todaysbride.com) requires you to register (complete with bride and groom's name; address, phone, wedding date) before you can access their planning tools. Once you get in, "My Planner" (see Figure 1) lets you enter your budget and actual amounts for 21 categories, much the same way Modernbride.com works.

A plus for Todaysbride.com: you have space to write notes and details for each budget item. For example, when you click on the dress, you can write in the bridal shop name, address, phone and contact not to mention the gown style number and other details. On the other hand, the allotted space is rather

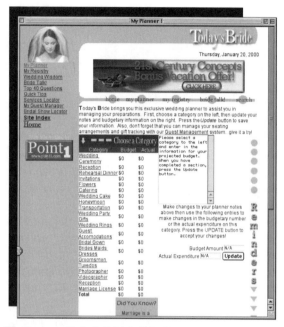

tiny for all that information.

"My Guest Manager" lets you enter in quite a lot of guest
info: address, phone, email, whether you sent an invitation,
reception table assignment, RSVP yes or no, shower gift, wedding gift and whether a thank you was sent. Nice, but we
found the page rather clunky to use in a test run.

❖ **The Knot.com.** The Knot has one of the best, most complete selections of planning tools of any site on the web. They
offer a "Big Day Budgeter," "Ultimate Wedding Checklist," and
a "Guest List Manager." These tools are among the best on the
Internet; we'll review them in-depth later in this chapter.

❖ **Weddingchannel.com.** Ditto for this site—their planning
tool are equal to or better than those of the Knot. We'll also
review this site in the "Best of the Web" section later in this
chapter.

❖ **Weddingbells.com.** Perhaps the most pathetic attempt at helping brides plan can be found on Weddingbell.com's web site. Once you find this area (choose Planning and Etiquette, then go to Planning Priorities) you'll find a screen that allows you to enter your general budget, the wedding's formality, number of guests, and lead time before your wedding date. Next you hit the button "Where do I start?" You'd expect to see some facts and figures show up like many of the other sites, but instead you get a page of very general advice. While the advice is fine, there is oddly no countdown checklist. At least the information is free and you don't have to register for it.

Red Flag

Watch out for what we call "etiquette breaches" with 'net planning tools. For example, on the Weddingnetwork.com's guest list manager, they offer to send out formal announcements of where you're registered to all the guests on your list (this is done via email or snail mail). Just because registries allow you to carpet bomb your guests with requests for goodies, it doesn't mean you *should*. Don't fall into the trap of letting sites use your guest list as advertising for their gift registries. Sending your guests an email that says, essentially, "BUY ME STUFF, HERE'S HOW!" is tacky. If they want to know where you're registered, they'll ask.

Best of the Web

The Knot.com
Web: www.theknot.com
What it is: Three killer tools to help plan your wedding, track your budget and manage a guest list.
What's Cool: We'll discuss each tool separately:

❖ In the **Big Day Budgeter** (www.theknot.com/budgeter-main.cgi, see Figure 2), you enter your wedding budget, number of guests and attendants. Then the site suggests a specific budget (they've taken national averages and percent breakdowns and scaled these to different budget figures) with breakdowns for ceremony, reception, attire, flowers, music and more. You can uncheck items that don't apply to your wedding and they'll recalculate the chart for you.

Another cool thing about the Knot's budgeter: it gives

Figure 2: The Knot's detailed "Budgeter" even gives you an idea about what budget figures might buy for each category.

you specifics on what you can afford. For example, if your dress budget is $1400, they tell you which designers make gowns in your price range. That's very cool.

Needs Work: The biggest problem with the Budgeter is it's not scaled by whether you are planning a wedding in a big or small city. For example, with a $20,000 budget, the Knot estimated we could buy a "sumptuous dinner buffet" at $30 a guest. That's all very well if your wedding is in Oklahoma City, but "sumptuous" isn't the word we'd use to describe a $30 wedding buffet in New York, Chicago or LA.

❖ The Knot's **Ultimate Wedding Checklist** (www.theknot.com/ checklist.cgi) is an impressive 200 item to-do list. You enter your wedding date and the site responds with appointments/tasks that should be accomplished each week before your wedding (you can view this list by the week so you don't get too over-whelmed). They also offer hyperlinks to relevant planning articles and you can add your own items to the checklist. We liked most of their specific planning advice (like a tip on ketubahs for Jewish weddings). Overall this checklist was impressive.

Needs Work: While we like the Checklist overall, some of the to do's are a bit self-serving such as: "Create a wedding web

Real Wedding Tip

COOKIES

How do wedding web sites like the Knot or the Wedding Channel know who you are when you use their planning tools? They use cookies, small files placed on your computer's hard drive that help web sites identify you when you visit. Cookies make it possible for you to return to a site and have it retrieve data like a guest list or planning calendar that you've set up in a previous visit.

Remember, it is possible to erase these cookies (under Preferences or Tools, most browsers will let you delete cookies)—and that might interfere with your ability to retrieve items like a guest list. Most browsers will let you control which cookies you accept. Consult your browser's help file if you want to adjust these settings.

page on the Knot." Another example: at 9-11 months, they recommend you start searching for a gown and of course "your best resource is Bridalsearch on the Knot." We kept waiting for Knot Task #264 to pop up, saying "Today, sit down and write out a check for your life savings to the Knot!" And while most of the advice is solid, we disagreed with some tips that, for example, suggested buying wedding insurance (an expensive frill that covers you in case your wedding is cancelled; few brides need this).

❖ **Guest List Manager** (www.theknot.com/guest-managerintro.cgi) is an excellent, one-stop location for compiling a guest list, recording RSVP's, mapping out seating charts for your reception and tracking gifts and thank you's. All you do is enter names, email addresses (optional) and the number of people in each party.

Later you can add more names and view the guest list at any time. And as you receive RSVP's you can adjust the number in the party, denote whether they are a guest of the bride or groom, on the A or B list and more.

There is an invitation page that allows you to enter all your guests' addresses, a seating page that helps you group guests into tables and a gift log page that tracks gifts including thank you's sent. All in all, very cool.

Needs Work: While the Guest List Manager has loads of features, it can be very complex—you'll need a high-speed Internet connection to get the most out of this tool. The Knot seems to sometimes be a victim of its own success—even with our speedy DSL connection, we were often left waiting for pages to appear.

We were also irked that the Guest List manager didn't have an "us" guest option—guests must either be assigned to the bride or groom category. Most couples have mutual friends (and parents may have their own group of friends), so this is one annoying omission. Finally, remember the Knot uses "cookie" technology to remember who you are—if you delete your cookie files from your browser, it may be difficult to recover the data. Be safe: keep a backup guest list in another program and print out your list (for safe keeping) every week or so. See the tip on page 38 for details on cookies.

THE WEDDINGCHANNEL.COM

Web: www.weddingchannel.com then go to planning. Under tools you'll see the budget planner.

What It Is: This budget planner not only calculates how much you can spend in each category, but also offers budgeting tips alongside the figures.

What's Cool: Like other online budget planners we tried, the Weddingchannel's version asks you to enter a budget level, number of guests and attendants, as well as your city and state. Then the budget planner produces an attractive list with budget figures and advice, all formatted with nifty little icons. If you don't need a category on the list, enter "0" and the form eliminates that category and recalculates the budget. Very nice.

Needs Work: While we like the idea of offering budgeting advice with the calculator function, some of the site's tips left us scratching our heads. For example, our mock budget came up with $600 for the wedding gown. Their tip for saving was to be sure to order the correct size so we wouldn't have to pay for alterations. Gee, thanks! Of course, whatever amount you spend on a gown, you should always order the right size. As if folks with a $2000 dress budget can just order a too-big dress because they can afford the alterations!

Also, despite the fact the Wedding Channel asks for the city and state you are getting married in, the budget planner

[Figure 3: Weddingchannel.com's snazzy budget planner is easy to use —but some of the advice left us wondering if the writer was one taco shy of a combo plate.]

on the site offers no regional customization. You get the same advice on spending whether you are getting married in New York City or Fargo, North Dakota.

WEDDINGNETWORK.COM

Web: www.weddingnetwork.com (click on Planning to access these tools.)

What it is: Four good planning tools keep you on budget and on schedule.

What's Cool: Each tool has its pluses and minuses:

❖ The **wedding budgeter** (see Figure 4 on the next page) on the Wedding Network is simple but effective. You enter an overall budget and the site then divides your spending into several categories automatically. It does allow you to add new categories, delete them or make comments for each entry on the list. You can enter your actual budget figures and the page will show you how much money you've saved from your estimated budget (how optimistic!).

Needs Work: Watch out for unnecessary items (no, not everyone needs or wants to purchase favors for their guests). Another negative: some of the figures seem a bit low. For a $10,000 wedding they suggested $165 for a wedding coordinator. Assuming you even need one, we doubt most wedding coordinators will work for that little of a fee.

❖ Wedding Network's **Task Scheduler** is an excellent calendar tool that allows you to generate an extensive to-do list of tasks. But it isn't just a count-down calendar. The tool allows you to add or delete tasks, show the whole list or parts of it (like this week, this month, completed or incomplete tasks, and more), sort by date, responsible party, and more. When you click on a specific task it takes you to a screen that allows you to customize the entry by changing the category or person responsible. You can even change the date and time of when the task needs to be completed. Whew! Off the scale on the coolness meter.

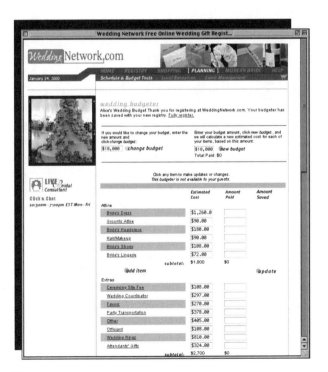

Figure 4: The Wedding Network's Budgeter is well organized, but watch out for unnecessary budget suggestions.

❖ The Wedding Network's **Event Scheduler** tracks engagement parties, bridal showers and bridesmaids luncheons. When you enter the address of the site where the event is being held, the Event Scheduler hyper links to a map generated by MapQuest.com—helpful if you want to print it out and send it to friends in the invitations. Plus you have a complete schedule of events arranged for you on the site.

❖ Finally, **Guest Management** is the last of the planning tools on this site. Wedding Network offers to help you tell your friends and family where you're registered. They give you three options: "Formal Announcements" that go to your guests four weeks before your wedding, insert cards for bridal shower invites or a "tactful email notification" of your registry choice. **Needs Work:** This is the most egregious example of what we noted earlier in the Red Flag section of this chapter. No matter how tactful the message may be, it is still considered in poor taste to solicit gifts from your wedding guests.

OTHER SITES TO CONSIDER

1 **Wedserv.com** (see Figure 5 on the next page) is a web site with free companion wedding planning software. You register at the site and then the company mails you a CD-ROM with the software (Windows only, there is no Mac version). All this is free; the software lets you do planning off-line and then interacts with the web site to provide budget checklists, instructional videos, and personal web site creation. They even have real humans who you can email or phone for support.

While this all sounds rather neat, we found the whole set-up to be rather cumbersome. After registering (where the site demands a large amount of personal information), you have to wait up to three WEEKS to get the CD-ROM. That's a long wait in the Internet world of "get it now, get it fast" web sites.

Once you get the software, you have to visit the site and get an "unlock code." All in all, quite a hassle.

2 **HudsonValleyWeddings.com** offers an informative budget breakdown as well as a basic "Who Pays for What" list at http://hudsonvalleyweddings.com/guide/budget.htm. The site even throws in some money saving tips for budget minded brides.

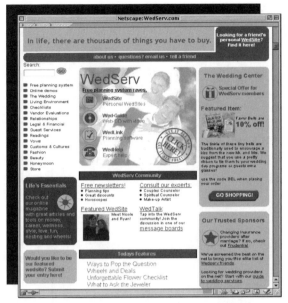

Netscape:WedServ.com

In life, there are thousands of things you have to buy.

Looking for a friend's personal WedSite? Find it here!

about us · questions? email us · tell a friend

Search:
[GO]

- Free planning system
- Online demos
- The Wedding
- Living Environment
- Checklists
- Vendor Evaluations
- Relationships
- Legal & Financial
- Guest Services
- Readings
- Vows
- Customs & Cultures
- Fashion
- Beauty
- Honeymoon
- Store

WedServ
Free planning system raves.

WedSite
Personal WedSites

Wed-Guide
Web CD with video

WedLink
Planning software

WedHelp
Expert help

WedServ Community

Free newsletters!
- Planning tips
- Great discounts
- Horoscopes

Consult our experts.
- Couples Counselor
- Spiritual Counselor
- Make-up Artist

Featured WedSite
Meet Nicole and Ryan!

WedTalk
Tap into the WedServ community! Join the discussion in one of our message boards

Todays Features
Ways to Pop the Question
Wheels and Deals
Unforgettable Flower Checklist
What to Ask the Jeweler

The Wedding Center

Special Offer for WedServ members

Featured Item:

Favor Bells are 10% off!

The tinkle of these tiny bells are traditionally used to encourage a kiss from the new Mr. and Mrs. We suggest that you use a pretty ribbon to tie them to your wedding day programs or guests wine glasses!

use the code BEL when placing your order

[GO SHOPPING!]

Our Trusted Sponsors

Changing insurance providers after marriage? If so, check out Prudential.

We've screened the best on the net to bring you this elite list of WedServ friends.

Looking for wedding providers on the net? Start with our guide to wedding services

Life's Essentials
Check out our online magazine with great articles and tools on money, career, wellness, style, love, fun, nesting and wheels!

Would you like to be our featured wedsite? Submit your entry here!

> Figure 5: WedServ is a hybrid: part CD-ROM, part web site. Their free software (Windows only) offers budget and guest list tools and interacts with their web site.

3 **Weddingshowroom.com** has a simple budget worksheet option (www.weddingshowroom.com/weddingshowroom/ budget.html) that allows brides to fill in totals. Although it's not interactive, it is a useful tool.

4 South Africa-based **Wedding Solutions** (www.wedding. co.za/9806/articles/WBudgets.htm) includes an online budget calculator that adds up amounts for each section, but doesn't give a grand total. You'll also find a "Who Pays for What" section on this site.

5 **1800Wedding.com** (www.1800wedding.com, see Figure 6 on the next page) offers four excellent planning tools to registered users—a calendar to track bridal appointments and to-do lists, an excellent budgeter with category breakdowns, guest list RSVP tool and "wedding party manager" to assign tasks and track responsibilities of various wedding party members. The design of this site is excellent and the tools are quite easy to use. Best of all, this site is free from the many annoying banner ads and sales pitches you see on other sites.

Figure 6: 1800wedding.com features four planning tools, including a "Wedding Party Manager" to whip those bridesmaids into shape.

WEDDING PLANNING SOFTWARE

Software for planning weddings comes in three flavors: pay, free, or shareware. Shareware lets you try it before paying a fee (on the honor system, typically). Many pay software companies offer free demo versions you can try.

- ❖ **Bride's Mate** www.bridesmate.com. A dealer for Carlson Craft invitations offers this free planning software for Windows.
- ❖ **I Thee Web** (www.itheeweb.com) is a great page with links to both free and pay wedding planning software for Windows or Mac.
- ❖ **My Wedding Companion** from Five Star Software (www.fivestarsoftware.com) offers a free trail offer for a $35 software package that includes such functions as Guest Manager, Budget Manager, TaskList Manager, Worksheets, reports and more.
- ❖ **Wedding Concierge** (www.weddingconcierge.com) offers free Guest List Manager software for Windows 95 users.

❖ **Wedding Magic** has a free demo version you can download from the Knot's Bridalink store (www.bridalink.com/store2/ magic.htm) for Windows 3.1 or Windows 95. This CD-ROM includes a guest database, budget and expense tracking, auto-scheduler, gifts/thank-you's and more. Price: $32.95.

TIPS AND TRICKS

1 **Don't rely on just one planning tool.** Sample several of the sites' budget tools to help fine tune your budget. You may find that a simple spread sheet program is as helpful as anything you can find on line.

2 **Consider general calendar web sites to manage wedding appointments.** If you want to track a wedding to-do list, consider sites like When.com (www.when.com). You can view your calendar by date, week or month. You can make the calendar open for a group of bridesmaids to see or just you and your fiancé.

FOR BETTER OR WORSE

So, is the Internet better at planning weddings than an old-fashioned spiral bound wedding planner? While we like the powerful interactive tools for budgets and guest lists on the Knot and Wedding Channel, we couldn't help but notice the advantages of a plain-old printed planner: you can keep your notes, appointments and printed material like contracts in one place. Best of all, you can take it with you—try to lug your laptop with wireless modem to a florist and you'll see the point. Until the web becomes truly wireless (where you can access all this data on the go instead of it being locked on your desktop computer), these 'net wedding planning tools may be of limited benefit. Bottom line: the web has some cool tools, but that won't eliminate a "place for your stuff."

Even if you stick with pencil and paper (or a spreadsheet) for your budget, the web still holds promise for communicating with your guests. In the next chapter, we'll show you how to create a personal wedding web page for free.

Create:

Whip up a free personal wedding page in seconds.

Yes, it is fun to chat with other brides and look up live web cams at remote honeymoon spots in the South Pacific—but is there something truly useful you can do with the Internet or your computer for your wedding?

In fact, there is: you can CREATE a personal web page that tells your wedding guests all the facts and figures about your wedding. This chapter will tell you how to do that for free in just minutes.

But that's not all: how about creating a wedding invitation on your computer and printing it out on nice-looking stock paper from your desktop printer? You don't have to be an expert graphic artists to do this—just check out a $20 software program that even includes the heavy card stock to print your invitations on. We'll discuss this at the end of this chapter.

How it Works

This chapter will discuss two types of "create your own web-sites:" those hosted by wedding web sites like the Wedding Channel and others hosted by web site companies that offer "general" sites. Either way, the process of creating a personal web site is rather the same. The good news: you don't have to know HTML (the programming language of web heads) to create your own site. There are four basic steps:

1 Register. Most sites require you to register (or "create an account") to create a personal wedding web page. Typically, that means providing your names and an email address and selecting a password (you must enter this to change your site so just any hacker can't play with it).

2 Enter the info. From there, you just follow the directions and enter various details about your wedding. These could include the story of how you met, wedding logistics, guest information (accommodations info for out-of-towners, etc.) and other details. Basically, this is a lot of typing. Some of the web sites we recommend have tools to make this easier, but still expect to have sore fingers in the end.

3 Give out the address to your friends. That's it: you tell your friends where to go to find the page and poof! Instant bridal community!

4 Change it whenever you want. Most personal wedding pages can be edited at any time to update information on the wedding, etc.

REALITY CHECK

❖ **How tech-savvy are your guests?** Yes, you may be addicted to the web, but remember that all those aunts, uncles and cousins may not be so wired. Keep in mind that you'll have to provide alternatives for those who don't have 'net connections to get out-of-town guest info, etc. (One low-tech answer: send a wedding newsletter to your friends with such info. A one-page letter can provide accommodations info and other details.)

❖ **Ads ahead.** Many of the wedding web sites we recommend in this chapter are free—but they may place ads (subtle and not-so-subtle) on "your" web page. Some of these ads take the form of banners or pop-up sales pitches. Others are more subtle—sites like the Wedding Channel sneak in text plugs for their gift registry (The Wedding Channel is pleased to inform you that Mary and John's wedding gift registry is online here!).

WISH LIST

1 **More security.** We found only some of the personal web sites on the Internet offered password protection. Adding this feature should be easy and user-friendly for couples that want to protect their privacy.

2 **Additional customization.** As you'll read later in this chapter, many free (non-wedding) web site services offer impressive customization abilities. It would be great if the wedding web sites offered more options like this.

RED FLAGS

Give details about your wedding on a personal web page at your own risk. In the mid 1990's, a string of residential robberies in Arkansas all had a common theme: they were the homes of brides and grooms (and their parents) and the burglaries all occurred during the wedding. How did these crooks now what homes to target? They just looked at the newspaper wedding announcements, which provided handy details such as the name of the bride and groom and the time of the ceremony. A simple search of the local phone book provided the home addresses.

Now, we don't tell you this story to scare you—but it is important to realize that when you broadcast your wedding details to the immediate world (via the newspaper or the Internet), you might open yourself (and your home) up to thieves. Think about it: you are basically advertising you won't be home for several hours during one specific day.

We suppose this might be more of an issue with high-crime urban areas than other towns. But residential burglaries can happen in communities both large and small.

How easy is it to look up personal wedding web pages on the Internet? Very easy, as it turns out. The Knot provides a handy list of couples by state. The Wedding Channel is a bit more discrete, requiring you to enter the name of the bride or groom before you can get all the info.

If you have security concerns about this information, you may want to "password protect" the page (requiring your guests to enter some password to gain access to sensitive details). That's an option with some web sites such as the Knot.

![Create]

THE BIG SEVEN

Only two of the Big Seven wedding web sites offer this service: the Knot and the Wedding Channel. Here's what each offers:

❖ **The Knot.** It's free and it's fancy-looking; the Knot's "Personal Wedding Web Page" is a three page web page that's easy to set up. The first (or home) page includes details about the bride and groom, how you met, how you were engaged and basic details about the wedding (where, when, etc). The second page (Details) gives more specific details on the wedding—the exact time, location, attire, menu, information on lodging and transportation. Good news: this page can be password-protected to limit access to just friends and family. The final page (Guestbook) is a private message board for you and your guests. Post messages here with additional info on your wedding or let guests trade messages about the event.

Figure 1: The Knot's personal wedding pages do allow for password protection.

Like everything with the Knot, the Personal Wedding Web pages are well designed with nice graphics that can even include pictures. But. . . the customization options are rather limited compared to other sites. The Knot's web pages lack other "interactive features" (like maps to the ceremony location) you'll read about later in this chapter.

❖ **The Wedding Channel.** Also free, the Wedding Channel offers simple personal wedding web pages that are free and customizable. First you must register with the site (also free), providing such basic info as the bride and groom's name, email, etc. Then you create the "Couples Profile Page." (The Wedding Channel has several sample pages that give you an idea of what to include). The profile includes bride and groom background, how you got engaged and a listing of various wedding attendants (bridesmaids, groomsmen, flower girl, etc). Additional wedding details can fill the bottom of the page, which can be customized with a picture of the couple.

Figure 2: The Wedding Channel's personal web pages are easy to set up and offer more customization options than the Knot.

The second page is "Wedding Logistics"—here you enter details about the location of the ceremony and reception. You can even add a map of the ceremony and reception locations, which is handy. The final page is the "Out of Town Guest Information" area, with travel arrangements (hotel, car, etc.).

In the "cool-ness" race, we'd have to give the edge to the Wedding Channel. The site lets you pick a type style and background color, add maps and even send an email to the couple. True, the Wedding Channel omits the password protection and "guestbook" features the Knot has, but we liked how the Wedding Channel formats the pages better than the Knot (two columns, etc.).

A chart at the bottom of this page compares and contrasts the personal wedding page offerings of the Knot and the Wedding Channel, plus two other options discussed later in this chapter.

WEB PAGE OPTIONS

These four sites offer personal wedding pages. Each is free, but they vary as to the number of pages offered, level of security and customization. Here's how they stack up:

Site	#Pages	Password?*	Customization**
The Knot	3	Yes	Good
Wedding Channel	3	No	Better
1800wedding .com	5	Yes	Good
Homestead .com	Unlimited	Yes	Best

Key:

*Password: does the site offer password protection?

** Our opinion of how customizable the site's offerings are.

BEST OF THE WEB

ECIRCLES
Web: www.ecircles.com

What it is: A digital hangout for your friends and family to share wedding info.

What's Cool: Just about everything. This site lets you set-up virtual "circles" of family and friends to help plan your wedding. Once inside the circle, you can use bulletin boards, set up chat rooms (text or voice), post photo albums, store files and more. Even more cool: you can set up multiple circles (such as one for just the bridesmaids, others for the groomsmen and another general one for all guests). Set-up is simple—you just tell the web site who to invite and they email invitations automatically. All this is free—if your guests use an optional shopping service to purchase gifts on your wish list, Ecircles makes money. But that's purely optional.

Needs work: This site might be best for smaller weddings (say under 100 or so guests). Managing a circle with 200 or 300 guests might be a bit much.

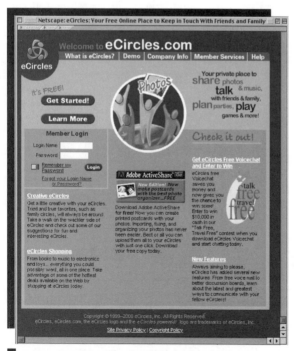

Figure 3: While not designed specifically for weddings, Ecircles is a great way to share info on a wedding, pictures, and more.

Another note: Ecircles requires plug-ins to make the most of certain features. You can download Adobe ActiveShare (free, of course) to help organize pictures and FireTalk to do the chats. This isn't that difficult to do (the site walks you though the procedures), but might be a bit intimidating for non-techie folks. Of course, Ecircles isn't designed specifically for weddings, so you might have to fiddle with the site to get it to do what you want. But it is a cool way to create a virtual community.

HOMESTEAD

Web: www.homestead.com

What it is: A powerful free web site service.

What's cool: Did we mention it's free? Homestead has easy-to-use templates that let you create amazing web pages, all in just minutes. "Elements" are wonderful add-ons that let you add preprogrammed items like guest books, chat rooms, images, or (my favorite) weather forecasts. How about a voice greeting from you and your fiancé welcoming guests? Or a web cam from the city where the wedding will be? It's all drag and drop to add these functions to your web page—nothing could be easier. You can begin with a pre-built page or start from scratch. Your web-

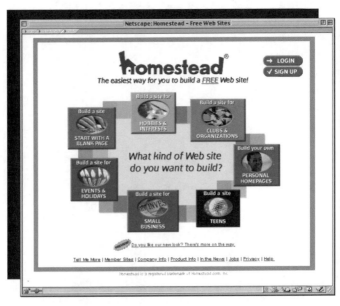

Figure 4: Homestead offers powerful "elements" to make it's free web sites ultra-cool. Click on "Events & Holidays" to start building a wedding web site.

site is accessed by entering something like www.yourname. homestead.com. You can work online or offline—there's even a downloadable version of Homestead that works offline. How does Homestead make money? Some of the elements are linked to other web sites (like Amazon), who pay Homestead for the free advertising.

Needs work: It would be nice if there were more wedding templates on line—we just saw a brief demo what you can do in the generic "events" category.

❖ **Runner-up.** In addition to Ecircles and Homestead, we should give kudos to another free wedding web site provider: 1800Wedding.com. The site walks you through a five-step process to create a site, including the basics about the event and options such as password protection. Unfortunately, there are no samples of what the finished pages look like, so creating a page on this site is a leap in the dark.

❖ **Pay sites.** If you want something more elaborate then the free sites mentioned earlier in this chapter, consider the following alternatives.

Wedding Web Sites (www.wedding-websites.com) offers extensive, customized wedding web sites—you can have a slideshow of baby pictures of the bride and groom, fade-in text, graphics and more. Yet, when we emailed the site to get a price list our email was bounced back as "undeliverable."

The Wedding Day (www.theweddingday.net) offers five professionally designed pages for $300. Other more elaborate packages run $600 to $1000 for additional pages, pictures and other extras. We thought the graphics on these pages were very professional, but the price is quite high.

Looking ideas for your wedding web page? **Ultimate Wedding.com** has a "web ring" where you can find over 300 wedding web sites created by brides and grooms. (A web ring is a group of related sites banded together to form linked circles. Their purpose: to allow more visitors to reach them quickly and easily). The specific address for the ring is www.ultimatewedding.com/webring.htm.

INVITATIONS

This article was first printed in our Bridal Bargains book.

Like the idea of doing your invitations yourself on a computer, but feel a bit intimidated? After all, maybe you're not a graphic artist. Even if you could track down laser-compatible invitation paper, what's the correct way to word an invitations, etiquette-wise?

We found a great answer to those questions: the Wedding Invitation kit, a CD-ROM software package from the Creative Card Company (a division of PC Papers and American Pad & Paper). This handy software program is available nationwide in office supply stores like Staples and Office Depot for about $20 (call 888-727-3772 for a store near you; web: www.pcpapers.com).

If you've got a Windows PC (version 3.1 or later) and a laser or ink jet printer, that's all you need to print out professional-looking invites. The CD-ROM guides you through the process of setting up an invitation—you enter the bride and groom's names, the date, location and other details . . . and the computer words the invitation in perfect etiquette.

Best of all, the kit contains heavyweight-paper stock to print 25 invitations, 25 envelopes, 50 "accessory folders" (for reception cards, response cards, maps, etc.), 50 companion envelopes for the accessory folders and several sample sheets to verify the printing. There are several invitation designs available and you can order refill packages in case you need more than 25 invitations. You can choose from five fonts (various cursive typestyles) and eight colors; there's even module to track gift information and keep a count of guests who will be attending the wedding.

We were skeptical about this concept until we actually saw some samples—they were impressive. The card stock is equivalent to what's available from mail order catalogs and the typefaces look very professional. The only bummer: there is no Mac version of the kit; Windows only. Of course, the quality of your printer may also affect your results. While the typefaces are excellent, the printing isn't raised (as you'd get from mail order or a stationary store). If you can live with that trade-off, than you'll love this software.

"My laser printer did such a beautiful job, you would never know it wasn't done by a professional," a reader told us

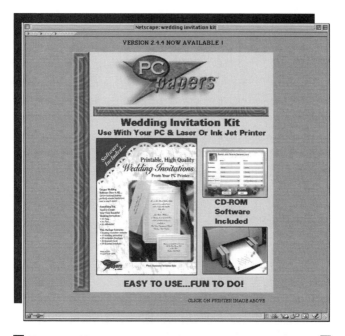

Figure 5: PC Papers "Wedding Invitations Kit" is a steal:
use your own computer to print out professional-looking
invites at a fraction of the cost.

after using the Wedding Invitation kit. "Total cost? $42. I fig-
ure the same design from a mail order catalog would have
been close to $200."

BRIDAL CRAFTS

Bridal Craft magazine offers ideas for veils and headpieces,
favors and other do-it-youself ideas. Their web site
(www.bridalcrafts.com) includes links to other craft info on
the web. Each issue of the magazine is $4.95.

FOR BETTER OR WORSE

Sure, it sounds so cool: a personal web site dedicated to your wedding, with such whiz-bang
features as an electronic guest book, online map
and more. But, let's cut through the digital hype and ask the
key question: does it really matter?

In the old days, folks just sent out wedding invitations
and guests had to find their way to the event. That meant

that out-of-towners had to arrange for travel and hotel accommodations on their own. At most, the bride and groom might have sent out a "save the date" letter before the wedding that detailed such travel arrangements; or they might have stuffed a map into the wedding invitation.

So, a personal wedding web site does help guests. But how much? And how do your guests figure out just where your website is? We suppose you send them an email (if you know their email addresses) or a letter via snail mail. But then what's the point? You haven't saved the first-class postage and effort to mail off 100 or 200 letters.

And what about your Aunt Minnie or Uncle Joe who don't have web access? Or guests who still have computers with Windows 1.0? All the techno wizardry may be lost on them.

The bottom line: personal wedding web sites are the most beneficial for weddings with large numbers of out-of-town guests (or those with far-flung bridesmaids). And it would help if a large percentage of those guests were web-savvy. For other weddings, this might be a case of 'net hype exceeding any real benefit.

Found a creative way to use the web to communicate with your guests? Think of a new spin on personal wedding web pages? Send us an email with your thoughts. See the "How to Reach Us" page at the end of this book for our contact information!

Find:

Need a DJ? Photographer? Baker? Use the 'net to discover local wedding merchants.

Forgive us if we wax nostalgic about this topic: helping brides find the best local wedding merchants brings back memories for us.

Our very first book, *Austin Weddings* was published way back in 1987 B.I. (that is, Before Internet). Back then, planning a wedding (and writing a book) was done the old-fashioned way. We jumped into our Honda Accord hatchback and cruised the city to visit wedding photographers, taste cakes and try on wedding gowns (Denise liked trying on the gowns too). We designed the whole thing on a Mac SE with Pagemaker 1.0 and the resulting 108 page book looked so amateurish, we've since had all the copies rounded up and burned.

The lesson this taught us, though, is that finding the perfect florist, caterer or reception site, is the Holy Grail of wedding planning. Look at all those pretty dress pictures in bridal magazines all you want, but if you can't find a decent gown shop with reasonable prices and good customer service, then you might as well forget it.

Like everything else, the Internet has transformed the process of finding local wedding vendors. In the old days, brides merely had the Yellow Pages and friends to help them with their wedding planning. Today with a few clicks of a mouse, you can access databases and find wedding photographers, bakers, florists and more.

Is it any better than our Honda hatchback? Read on.

How It Works

We've found four basic places on the 'net that catalog all the best (and worst?) of the wedding industry:

1 Wedding vendor databases. These databases are most numerous on the Big 7 sites and allow you to search by city and state or zip (or area) codes. For example, the WeddingChannel.com give you a choice of entering a zip code or a city/state. Then you click on an icon for different categories of vendors to find listings in your area. In some cases, the site will have a link to the vendor's web site.

[Figure 1: Type in your zip code or city and state to find local vendors at the WeddingChannel.com's colorful local vendor site.]

2 **Merchant associations.** Yes, there is an association for just about any profession and weddings are no exception. You'll find videographer associations, groups of caterers and photographers and more. The best news: most of these groups have web pages where you can look up members or request they contact you.

3 **Message boards and newsgroups.** These "community" sites (see Chapter 7 for more details) are often used by brides looking for a specific vendor or location for their wedding. Although this is more hit or miss depending on how well traveled the message board is, you can sometimes zero in on a particular request. For example, if you're trying to locate a vintage clothing store in San Diego selling antique wedding gowns, you could post to a message board or newsgroup and other San Diego brides can give you a referral. Unlike other "vendor search sites" that are larded with advertisements, the message boards let you cut through the clutter and get the answer you are looking for (sometimes). Another plus: brides and grooms are often frank in sharing their opinions about the best and worst businesses.

4 **City guides and directories.** These sites are designed as portals or directories to the vast number of city specific web sites out there. We'll suggest several that you can use as a jumping off point to find other pages with directories of possible reception locations and other local merchants.

REALITY CHECK

❖ **Some of the info can be out of date.** In researching this book, we've discovered web sites don't update their local listings with any regularity. That means you could be spending your time chasing vendors who don't exist or have moved and changed their phone numbers. Yeah, we realize that many web sites have a limited staff that has to manage huge amounts of data—but we're still dismayed by the incorrect or out-of-date info out there. Our guess: as many as 20% of the listings are NOT current.

❖ **Pay to play.** As we mentioned in chapter 2, the Knot offers a nifty local photographer search engine (see Figure 2 on the next page). You pop in your area code, budget and type of

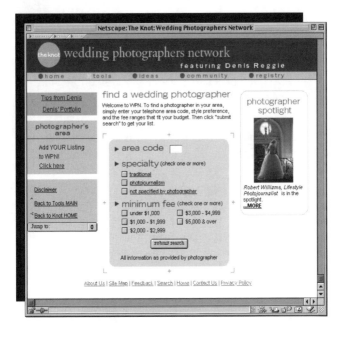

Figure 2: Pop in your area code and budget and the Knot will suggest photographers for you—but only those who've paid the Knot up to $720 bucks a year.

photographer you're looking for. Then the Knot generates a handy list of photographers' web sites and, in some cases, an online portfolio. What the Knot "forgets" to mention to their users is they charge photographers up to $720 a year to get "top priority" in the search results. The fact that they don't disclose this is rather shameful, but a quick lesson in the blurred lines between editorial and advertising on the net. A word to the wise: be aware that any site's top recommended vendors may have paid to be there.

❖ **More ad money than brains.** We've noticed many wedding vendors listed in these databases may NOT be the cream of the crop. Some of the heaviest advertisers are young companies without established track records. Others are high-volume shops that need a steady supply of new brides to keep running. By contrast, the very best wedding professionals in many cities are so busy they advertise only by word of mouth—they may never show up on these vendor lists.

WISH LIST

Despite the many advantages of the web when it comes to finding local vendors, there is always room for improvement. Our wish list:

1 More maps. Many of these wedding directories don't have decent maps to stores, sites and other vendors. How hard is it to link up with an online site map site to do this (like MapQuest.com)?

2 More *Consumer Reports*-style information. We know it might be wishful thinking, but wouldn't it be great if brides were able to post reviews of merchants for different locales (sort of like how readers post mini-book reviews on Amazon.com)? We realize this wish runs headlong into web sites' attempts to attract advertising, but it would be truly helpful to brides to know details such as a particular florist only works with high end clients or this baker takes three weeks to schedule an appointment. This kind of real life information is lacking today.

THE BIG SEVEN

It's hit or miss when it comes to finding local vendors on the seven largest wedding web sites. Here is an overview:

❖ **The Knot** (www.theknot.com) offers a "Vendor Finder" page in association with the Wedding Pages, an ad-based local wedding magazine (now a subsidary of the Knot). Once you call up the vendor finder, you can choose your city or state and then you jump to a screen with categories. If you choose a category like wedding attire, you'll find listings of bridal shops and formal wear stores in your area. Some stores have links to a description page or even their own web site.

Of course, this is all advertising. The Wedding Pages is like a bridal Yellow Pages: businesses pay for listings. The folks with additional links merely pay more than those with simple line listings. While this may be a great starting point to gather a few names, don't rely on the Knot to find the crème de la crème out there.

Separate from the Vendor Finder is the Knot's Wedding

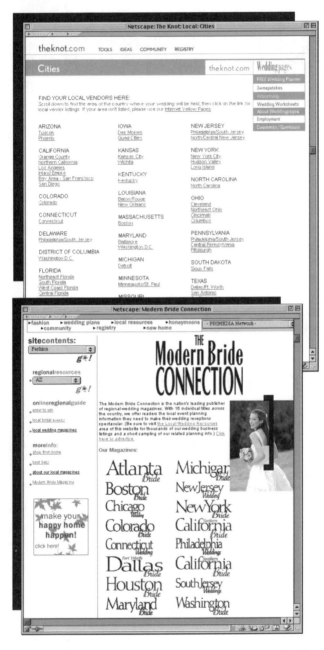

Figure 3: A sampling of the local vendor pages on the Knot and ModernBride.com. The Knot spent $8 million to acquire the Wedding Pages in 2000 to beef up their local listings page. Meanwhile, Modern Bride relies on its 14 regional bridal magazines to provide content for its local vendor section.

Photographers Network. Enter an area code, specify a budget and pick a photography style and then the site gives you a limited list of photographers. Make that VERY limited list. When we searched for photographers in our area code (303) we received a list of only 14 for the whole Denver metro area. On top of that, the first five listings were for photographers as far away as New York and Washington state! (As we noted earlier in this chapter, photographers pay a premium to be listed in this directory).

❖ **Modern Bride** (www.modernbride.com) also owns 14 regional wedding magazines for Atlanta, Boston, Chicago, Colorado, Connecticut, Maryland, Michigan, New Jersey, New York, Northern California, Philadelphia, Southern California, South Jersey and Washington DC. If you happen to be planning a wedding in one of those locations, you'll find quite a bit of information on local resources.

We found vendor listings on this site that included basic contact information, a couple sentence description and (in some cases) a link to the businesses web site. Beyond the listings of local businesses, the site also offers tips on honeymooning in the region, info on getting a marriage license, newspaper announcement advice and local wedding events. One plus: this site is very easy to navigate.

If you live in an area NOT covered by one of the regional magazines mentioned above, you'll find substantially less information on this site. For example, we checked out Iowa and found resource listings for only Bridal Registries, Invitations and a few other non site-specific services.

❖ **Bliss** (www.blissezine.com) doesn't offer much in the way of regional or local vendor lists but they do have some links (www.blissezine.com/library/reception.asp) to merchant associations or directories like the American Disc Jockey Association. You'll also find links to individual web sites for businesses at various locations on the site. It takes some effort to uncover this info, however.

❖ **Wedding Channel** (www.weddingchannel.com) has a nicely-arranged local vendor area (see Figure 1 earlier in this chapter). Pop in your city or zip code and you get a page with various category choices. The listings are rather comprehensive. On a random check for florists in Phoenix, we found 80 listings. Some were outside the metro area in other parts of Arizona, but that was rather impressive. In some cases, florists had a link to a description page with a bit more info (and perhaps a link to the vendor's web site).

Brides planning in smaller cities might be out of luck with the Wedding Channel, however. A search for Madison, Wisconsin wedding vendors turned up many listings for Chicago reception sites, but we thought that was a bit far to drive.

❖ **WeddingBells.com** claims to offer local wedding vendor information . . . but when you click on the button, you'll find yourself limited to only six cities (Boston, Chicago, Dallas/Ft.Worth, Los Angeles, New York and San Francisco). Presumably, more locations will be added in the future, but the pickings were slim on our visit. Even if you live in one of these six cities, you can only surf listings for gift registries, reception venues/caterers, wedding fashions and wedding supplies/services.

Once you choose a category (and sub-category in some cases), you find a well organized listing of vendors including email addresses and web sites (if available). Our sampling of San Francisco bridal shops turned up just four listings in the entire Bay Area.

❖ **Wednet.com** offers a rather crude Wedding Vendors option on their site. Once you hit the button, the site yields you a chart of the fifty states to choose from. Click on a state, and the

How local is local?

Five of the big seven wedding web sites say they can help you find local wedding vendors. Here's how they stack up:

Site	# Cities	Search Method	Our Take
The Knot	Nationwide	By City/State	Average
Modern Bride	14 regions	State	Average
WeddingChannel	Nationwide	City/State or Zip	Excellent
WeddingBells	6 cities	City	Poor
WedNet	Nationwide	State	Poor

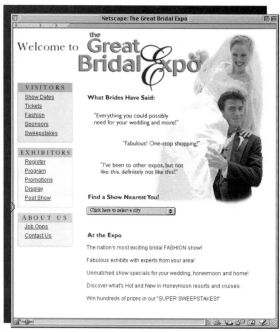

Welcome to **the Great Bridal Expo**

VISITORS
Show Dates
Tickets
Fashion
Sponsors
Sweepstakes

EXHIBITORS
Register
Program
Promotions
Display
Post Show

ABOUT US
Job Opps
Contact Us

What Brides Have Said:

"Everything you could possibly
need for your wedding and more!"

"Fabulous! One-stop shopping!"

"I've been to other expos, but not
like this, definitely not like this!"

Find a Show Nearest You!

Click here to select a city

At the Expo

The nation's most exciting bridal FASHION show!

Fabulous exhibits with experts from your area!

Unmatched show specials for your wedding, honeymoon and home!

Discover what's Hot and New in Honeymoon resorts and cruises.

Win hundreds of prizes in our "SUPER SWEEPSTAKES!"

Figure 4: The Great Bridal Expo's site lists upcoming shows in 14 cities—and you order tickets ($7 each) online with a credit card. The only bummer: some of the show info is out of date.

resulting page is merely a listing of vendors by category—and not a very pretty one at that. Some listings have a symbol telling you they have a web site and offering a hyperlink to it. Other listings merely offer the basic information about the business. This site might be helpful for brides in small states like Rhode Island, but forget sifting through the Texas or California listings unless you have plenty of time on your hands.

❖ Bridal shows are a good place to find vendors, if you can stand all the commercial hucksterism at such events. **TodaysBride.com** offers a bridal show locator with over 1000 events. But to get that info, you've got to give up a load of personal information (including home address and phone numbers). A side note: this site is apparently building a local vendor database, but it was only "under construction" as we went to press.

Another source for bridal shows: Modern Bride's **"Great Bridal Expo"** (www.greatbridalexpo.com) hosts shows nation wide. Their site includes a calendar of upcoming shows. Another source: you can usually find several local shows by just looking in your local newspaper.

Red Flags

Watch out for sites that require you to enter large amounts of information about your wedding before you can get a referral to local vendors. For example, the Wedding and Event Videographers' Association (WEVA) web site asks you to enter where you are getting married and how many guests you're expecting. Then the site broadcasts this to local videographers who are supposed to contact you (see Figure 5 below).

The problem? We know wedding merchants like to "cherry pick" their customers, hoping to lure brides with fat wallets. If merchants know you are planning a smaller wedding at a budget location, they may never contact you. Even if you planned to spend a fortune on wedding videography, you may find yourself without any calls from vendors, singing the country tune "If the phone don't ring, it's me."

A better bet: just contact the national or regional headquarters of an association by phone or email. Most are happy to give you a list of members in your area, no questions asked.

Figure 5: The Wedding and Event Videographers Association lets its members cherry-pick brides, thanks to the detailed information on your wedding WEVA requests on their referral form.

BEST OF THE WEB

Ironically, we found the best places to find local wedding vendors were NOT sites that had "weddings" in their address. Instead, we thought the best tools were some of the city directories that are "portals" with hundreds of links to other sites.

What can you find at these portals? The obvious biggie is sites for wedding ceremonies and receptions. Often these are tucked away under listings of meeting sites, historic homes, museums, and other facilities. Yes, this requires a bit of hunting and pecking to uncover, but we found these portals to be the most comprehensive local guides on the Internet:

❖ **Citysearch.com** has one of the easiest sites to use if you're looking for wedding information and local resources in about 40 different cities. The day we visited they even had a special wedding section called "Wedding Bells" featured on the site. But if you merely enter wedding into their key word search

Figure 6: CitySearch.com's "Wedding Bells" section includes the Matrimony Marketplace with local resource. Each section is customized by city (this one is for Denver).

function, the site generates a list of hundreds of reception sites, florists, photographers and more. We were impressed that many listings offer reviews (even "recommending" certain facilities!), as well as thumbnail photos, contact info and online maps. This site is a winner.

❖ **Digitalcities.com** allows you to access incredible information on 60+ cities. Check out their Visitor's Guide, Maps and Directions, Attractions, and Local Links sections to find ideas for reception sites, any local events going on during your wedding weekend and attractions for your out of town guests to enjoy.

❖ **Excite's** travel pages are another good option. You can access them through www.excite.com/travel. Although it takes a few clicks to get to a city, you can look up possible wedding and reception sites under such headings as What to Do, Where to Eat, Where to Stay, Specialty Guides and more. (Hint: remember that many restaurants have banquet rooms that cater to wedding receptions. Don't overlooks these listings, especially for restaurants that specialize in "special occasions").

❖ **Timeout.com** offers info on New York, Boston, Chicago, New Orleans and six other cities in the US. We found this site to be well-organized and easy to use.

❖ The goal of **USA Citylink** (www.usacitylink.com) is to help web surfers find local, municipal and other government web sites. Unlike other sites with info on a limited number of cities, you can use this site to access web sites for almost any town in any of the 50 states. Granted, there may not be a ton of entries under small, rural towns like Round Top, Texas, but even for this small burg we found several sites. Once you choose a city, you'll find lots of areas to research. Hint: try local Chamber of Commerce sites or local Visitor's/Tourism Bureau sites to get lists of "meeting facilities." These often double as reception sites in most towns.

❖ **Yahoo's** city guide (http://local.yahoo.com) allows you to keyword search a combination of both "weddings" and the city you are looking for. We came up with four categories including listings of photographers, videographers, and bridal shops for Austin, Texas when we searched the local site. Yahoo has one of the best search engines available.

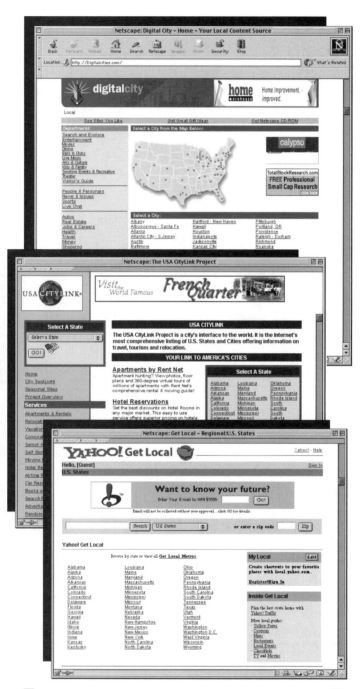

Figure 7: A sampling of the city "portals" from Digital City, USA CityLink and Yahoo. Each can help you discover hidden reception sites and other wedding vendors.

Professional Associations

Sure, these city directory sites are great to find unusual reception sites, but if you're looking for a specific vendor like a caterer, where can you go? Check out professional associations of photographers or caterers to help you find a local member or chapter in your town. Some sites actually give you a listing of members on line while others give you a phone number for your local chapter in your home town. (See Figure 7 on the next page for samples of these pages.) Examples include:

❖ **The Professional Association of Custom Clothiers** (http://paccprofessionals.org)

❖ **The National Association of Catering Executives** (www.nace.net)

❖ **Wedding and Event Videographers Associations** (www.weva.com)

❖ **June Wedding** (wedding consultants association). (www.junewedding.com)

❖ **The Professional Photographer Association** (www.ppa.com).

Other Sites to Consider

Some sites with local wedding vendor info aren't part of a large wedding web site or a professional association. Yet, they can still provide helpful info. A sampling:

❖ **1800wedding.com** shows a lot of promise. They've teamed up with a visual tour technology company called Bamboo.com to offer virtual tours of reception sites. As of this writing, the tours and vendor lists are only available to brides in Southern California. They expect to add 54 other locations in 2000.

What's cool about this site is you can take a virtual panoramic tour of reception sites. You can zoom in, change rooms and more. Very cool—if they line up more sites, this could be quite useful.

[Figure 7: Professional associations of seamstresses, caterers
and photographers all have great home pages where you
can access local member directories.]

❖ **ProDJ.com** (see Figure 8 below) is a terrific site that focuses on finding a DJ in the US or Canada. When you enter the easy-to-use site, you can immediately go to the search page and find a DJ. Some cities we searched returned as many as two dozen possibilities.

❖ **Weddinglinksgalore.com** is basically a jump site that links to other web sites. Under the reception category, some states had has many as five or six links. Search one of 24 categories, including photographers, caterers, florists, and more.

❖ **Smartbride.com** is another "coming soon" site. Their hook is to have brides review wedding vendors and services a la Amazon.com. The demo site that was up as of this writing looked promising.

❖ The California-based publishers of the book series **Here Comes the Guide** have now added a web site (www.here-comestheguide.com, see Figure 9 on the next page) that is easy to use and quite comprehensive. Enter the region you are interested in to find a reception site, site type, site view, and catering option and you get an amazing list of possibilities. Listings include photos and detailed info on the site's offerings. We only wish this site covered more than the Golden State.

Figure 8: It isn't much to look at, but ProDj.com has an extensive directory of disc jockeys in the U.S. and Canada.

Figure 9: Planning a wedding in California? Here Comes the Guide's site should be a must-visit in your search for a reception site.

FOR BETTER OR WORSE

It is still a leap of faith to trust the web to find you a reception site, caterer, florist or any other wedding vendor. Yes, you can uncover some possibilities you never thought of—and some sites show promise at providing useful consumer information. Yet, this will take some effort . . . we found surfing these sites for local wedding vendor info to be frustrating.

Your best bet is still to ask friends, family and other brides for references. Our time-honored tip: ask wedding merchants for referrals to other professionals they respect. This is still more effective than the web, in our opinion. Right now, the Internet for brides searching for local vendors is basically a glorified Yellow Pages with a slick digital interface.

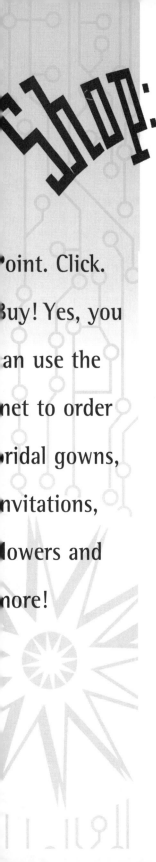

Shop:

Point. Click. Buy! Yes, you can use the net to order bridal gowns, invitations, flowers and more!

Unless you've lived on a remote South Pacific island for the last five years, you couldn't have escaped all the hype about "e-commerce," or simply put, buying stuff on the Internet. Sure, you can buy books, CD's or airline tickets online, but what about items for your wedding?

Not surprisingly, the answer is yes—with caveats, asterisks and a few "but's." For example, yes, you can buy a wedding gown or bridesmaids dress online and save some bucks—but the process is anything but easy right now. Yes, you can view and buy wedding invitations on the 'net—but you'll still probably need to order samples that will arrive via old-fashioned snail mail.

And so on. Perhaps the best thing about e-shopping for your wedding is the myriad of tchotchkes you can buy online. Let's face it—finding local stores that stock wedding favors, candles, cake toppers and other items that you'll only buy once in your life isn't that easy. The 'net lets you hook up with obscure companies that turn out unity candles, lacey garters and other necessary bridal equipment. In this chapter, we'll show you where to go to find gowns, invitations, accessories and more.

First, though, let's take a look at the types of e-shopping that exist today:

How it Works

Online merchants can roughly be divided into two categories: pure e-tailers and hybrid "clicks and mortar" stores/catalogs. A brief word on each:

1 E-tailers who exist solely on the web. Perhaps the most famous examples are Amazon and Etoys, but in a way, some of the Big Seven wedding web sites are e-tailers. Most of the major bridal sites have online stores that sell a stream of items, gadgets and doo-dads (see Figure 1). Like all e-commerce sites, you basically look at a picture of the item on the screen, click on an "order" button and zap! Your order goes off to the company and arrives by mail a few days later. At least that's how it's SUPPOSED to work. Later in this chapter, we'll list some Red Flags of e-shopping.

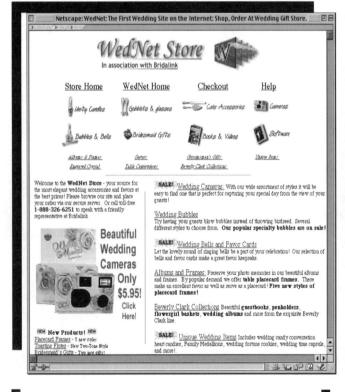

[Figure 1: Wednet hawks favors and wedding cameras, among other tchotchkes.]

Netscape:

Rexcraft

e | easiest™

Home | About Us | Contact Us | Invitations | Planning Tips

Welcome to Rexcraft!

We have more than 80 years of wedding experience and are one of the most trusted names in the industry. We've filled this site with a wide selection of invitations to help create the wedding of your dreams. Simply click the invitations link below to begin.

Invitations

Free Catalog

Satisfaction Guaranteed
You have enough to worry about in your life right now. That's why we guarantee every product that we offer. If you are not completely satisfied with any item simply return it within 30 days and we will replace the item or refund your money.

Free Gift
When you order over $100.00 of merchandise from Rexcraft, you'll receive our "From the Heart" glass keepsake box FREE. It's our way of saying "Thanks" for trusting us to make your wedding dreams come true.

Something traditional...
Something new...
Something colorful...
Something YOU!

[Figure 2: Rexcraft (www.rexcraft.com) sells invitations from both their catalog and web site.]

2 **Clicks and mortar.** Yes, a clever name to describe a hybrid business—a combo real-life retailer and a web site (hence the clicks and mortar . . . cute, eh?). In the wedding world, there are bridal retailers who've figured out enough HTML to open up a cyber-shop. They take orders for bridal gowns and bridesmaids dresses through the web. In a similar vein, invitation mail-order catalogs have online web sites that also let you view and order invites online.

So, this is all very cool. You'll just order your bridal gown, wedding flowers, invitations and other miscellaneous bridal stuff all in the comfort of your pajamas at 3am, right? Hold it. E-shopping in the bridal world isn't that easy. Let's look at the following reality check.

REALITY CHECK

E-shopping is a great convenience, but there are cautions. Consider these caveats:

❖ **Objects may be fuzzier than they appear.** Web sites are still figuring out how best to present products for sale online—often the pictures are not the best and the descriptions are lacking. In some cases, the graphics are not optimized for the web. That's a problem with products like a white bridal gown. If a web site simply scans a dress photo from a magazine or catalog, there is often a loss of detail. Subtle lace and beading are a blur. We actually saw one gown web site that used magazine pictures with a CREASE down the middle. The same problem happens with invitations: it's best to see a real-life sample of the paper before you plunk down your money. The bottom line: ordering a gown, invitation or other item just from a picture is risky. The Internet simply doesn't let you touch and feel products like you can in a real store.

❖ **Some retailers hate the 'net.** And they'll make it as difficult as possible for you to shop in a store but then order online. For instance, take bridal dress shops—please! We have complained about the practice of "tag-ripping" in bridal shops for ten years and nothing much has changed. In national surveys, we found three out of four (yes, 75%!) bridal shops remove manufacturer's tags (designer name, fiber content, country of origin, etc.) from their sample gowns. Why? Shops don't want you trying on a gown and then clicking your way to a major discount online. So, many will take extreme measures (both legal and illegal) to make sure they keep your dollars in their store.

If you try on a gown at a bridal shop that rips tags and refuses to identify the gown, is there any way of finding out the manufacturer and style number? Yes—if you can find a picture of the gown online or in a magazine. And that's a big IF. Not all bridal gowns or bridesmaids are pictured (in catalogs, online or in magazine ads). We'll have more tips on cyber dress shopping later in this chapter.

❖ **Some assembly may be required.** Bought a bridal gown online but the skirt needs to be shortened? Almost every bridal gown needs some alterations, whether a minor tuck or major surgery. If you order online, where do you go for alterations? We'll have some solutions later in this chapter, but it does point out that in-store alterations are darn convenient. Other bridal items you buy online may require some assembly as well. You can order flowers online at wholesale prices direct from a grower—but you (or a friend or relative) have to arrange them yourself. Mail-order invitations are great—but you may have to do some assembly (tie ribbons, stuff envelopes, add tissue paper). Some stationery retailers include these services as part of their package, which again is a nice perk.

Wish List

Many bridal e-commerce sites have a distinct "Version 1.0" feel to them—you get the feeling that many sites are thrown up quickly to capitalize on 'net hype, without much thought as to how user friendly they are. Topping our wish list includes:

1 **Online ordering.** This is especially a problem with gown sites. Want to order a dress online? With many sites, you can't. First, you email the site with a dress price quote request. Then some sites require you to call their store (some have toll-free numbers; others don't) during business hours to get the price quote. Want to place the order? Another phone call on your dime. Part of the problem: many gown manufacturers don't want retailers to quote prices over the 'net. They strong arm bridal shops into limiting their web site offerings. Bottom line: these manufacturer threats hobble e-commerce. We suspect this will improve over time,

Real Wedding Tip

E-commerce Lingo

Here are some terms you'll encounter when shopping online:

❖ *Email receipt: most sites will send you an email receipt upon ordering. Check the receipt to make sure the quantities and items are correct.*

❖ *Secure site: The best online shopping sites offer "secure servers" to make sure credit card and other information is securely transferred from your computer to the site. Look for the little "padlock" icon at the bottom of your browser window—if it is in the locked position, you are at a secure site.*

❖ *Shopping cart: Many sites let you add items to a virtual shopping cart and then head to a check out area.*

but for now it can be a pain to place online orders.

2 **Order tracking.** Even some of the Big 7 wedding sites don't offer this simplest convenience: the ability to track your order. Has it been shipped? Backordered? Canceled? It's hard to tell with some sites.

3 **More professionalism.** Surfing Amazon or Etoys makes us long for something similar for the wedding world. The bottom line: there is no "super site" to buy wedding items. That means surfers will have to content with amateur sites and all their vagaries for the time being.

THE BIG SEVEN

E-commerce has been the mantra of major wedding sites ever since the online advertising failed to live up to its initial hype. The result: these sites have morphed into virtual carnival barkers, hawking all manner of wedding stuff big and small. Here's an overview:

❖ **ModernBride.com.** This site has a hodge-podge of offerings. A click on the "Shop Online" button takes you to the ModernBride.com Marketplace, where you can buy such odd items as diet pills, fax machines and computer games. What this has to do with weddings is beyond us. A click on "Unique Gift" items takes you to their sister site Wedding Network (weddingnetwork.com) where you can shop local (by state) shops for bed & bath, home furnishings, home improvement and more.

❖ **The Knot** (theknot.com) is probably the most aggressive wedding site when it comes to e-commerce. A visit to the Knot Wedding Shop let's you browse such diverse items as wedding bubbles (an alternative to the traditional rice throw; choose from 12 different varieties) to ring pillows and unity candles. Single-use cameras seem to be a big-seller (at about $6 each) as well as all manner of bridesmaids gifts (heart mango gel candle at $13). The graphics are good and the site's shopping cart performs seamlessly.

❖ **Wednet's Store** (wednet.com) is a jumbled mess but there is a large variety of items—wedding cameras, bubbles, favors, albums, frames, goblets, gifts and more. Yeah, there is some kitsch here (Wedding Countdown Clock, bridal aromatherapy oils), but we like their low-price guarantee (if you see a lower price advertised, the site says they'll beat it). The only bummer: the online shopping cart feature wasn't working when we last visited.

Figure 3: Looking to buy wedding cameras? Cake accessories? Favors? The Knot and Wedding Channel both have online stores stocked with all manner of bridal accessories.

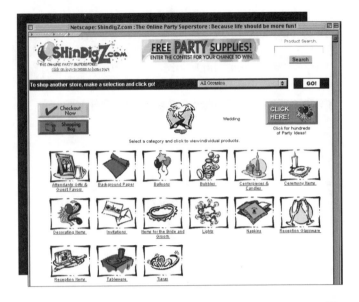

Netscape: ShindigZ.com : The Online Party Superstore : Because life should be more fun!

Figure 4: ShindigZ.com is an online party store with a large section dedicated to weddings and showers.

Another site to consider

❖ **ShindigZ** (www.shindigZ.com, see Figure 4 above) is an online party superstore. The company's colorful web site has a section for both weddings and bridal showers. We saw attendants gifts, invitations, decorating items, single-use cameras and even tiaras. Prices aren't the best—we noticed other sites had better deals. BUT, the site was offering free shipping for orders over $75 when we last visited and that might make the prices more attractive.

Red Flags

Before your whip out the credit card, beware of these caveats to 'net shopping:

1 **Shipping.** Before you get too excited about an online shopping bargain, don't forget to ask about shipping costs. And some sites make this difficult to determine—a few require you to wade through numerous screens of ordering information before you discover shipping charges. We wish more sites were up front. And remember that expedited (overnight) charges can be exorbitant. Plan ahead.

2 **Non-secure servers.** While most fears about online shopping have evaporated in the past year, there are still a few small wedding sites that do NOT use secure servers. That's Internet-speak for a technology that ensures your credit card number, address and phone are protected from hackers when beamed across the 'net. The bottom line: be sure to check for a secure server before placing an order. Look at the bottom of your browser and check for a small "pad lock" graphic that indicates a secure server is in use.

3 **Disappearing acts.** Just like in the physical world, web sites can go out of business with little warning. One bridal dress site, Milles Tendres, quit business in 1998 after taking dress orders from quite a few brides. Some of those consumers did not get their deposits back or had to scramble to line up an alternate source for their dress. Now, we don't mention this to scare you—the reality is this possibility is quite remote. And we've seen numerous cases of physical bridal retailers that have disappeared as well over the years, taking consumers dress deposits with them. Just be aware of the risks. And follow the "Tips & Tricks" section we have later in this chapter for some protection against scamsters.

Bridal Gowns: Not Quite Ready for Prime Time

Talk about your captive audiences: before the Internet, if you wanted to buy a bridal gown or bridesmaids dress, you had little choice—go visit your friendly "full service" bridal retailers and pay full retail. Since the shops that sell bridal apparel in one city or town are relatively limited, so was your choice.

Oh, you don't like what's offered in your town? Or the shops in your area don't carry the designer you've fallen in love with? Or you don't need or want "full service" from a shop, just the lowest price? Before the 'net, that was just tough. Unless you could travel by car or air to a nearby city, you were stuck. And the cost of an airline ticket to New York or Chicago typically outweighed any savings.

Mail-order pioneer, Baltimore-based **Discount Bridal Service** (www.discountbridalservice.com; see Figure 5 on the next page) and web sites like **PearlsPlace.com** changed all that. Now you do have a choice—stick with your local bridal retailer and hopefully get full service (and pay for it) or surf to savings online.

[Figure 5 Discount Bridal Service has 300+ dealers
nationwide who sell gowns and accessories at a discount.]

Of course, ordering a bridal gown or bridesmaids dress
isn't like buying a book or CD from Amazon. This requires
some real legwork on your part. After interviewing dozens of
brides who've successfully ordered dresses online, we've
developed several consumer tips to make this smoother.

TIPS & TRICKS TO BUYING A GOWN ONLINE

1 **Do your homework.** Browse magazines, visit
stores and scope out various styles of
gowns—do you want long or short sleeves? Ball
gown or A-line? The sheer variety of bridal gowns out there is
staggering; take some time to whittle down all the styles, sil-
houettes, fabric options and more. Later in this chapter, we'll
give you some general research sites to help you do this.

2 **Try it on first.** Okay, you've decided what will look best.
Now see how those gowns look in the real world. A dress
in a magazine is often a different proposition than one on a
real body in the real world. Keep an open mind—you may find
the "perfect" gown is not what you first thought. Trying on

the dress is key; while some brides order online without ever seeing their "dream dress," that's a risky proposition since all sales are non-refundable.

3 **Nail down the style number.** This is the trickiest part of online shopping—exactly *what* dress are you looking at? Most web sites can price quote a gown ONLY if you know one of three things: the true style number, where/when the dress was advertised in a magazine or a web page where you saw the dress. Since bridal retailers often hide style numbers (and manufacturer names), brides are left hunting for this information. One tip: find a picture of the dress in a magazine and web site and take this with you to the store, asking to see that SPECIFIC dress.

4 **See if the shop will match the price.** You might be surprised—many bridal retailers want to compete with the Internet. If you order multiple items (gown, headpiece, bridesmaids, etc.), your negotiating leverage is increased. If the shop won't match the price, see if they will throw in several extras (alterations, pressing, and so on) as freebies.

5 **Factor in all the "extras."** Speaking of alterations, remember you will have to line up a seamstress or find a place to alter your gown. Your dress may also have to be steamed or pressed prior to the wedding. Price the gown at retail with all those services and then compare that to the online deal.

6 **Leave plenty of time.** Many mail order or 'net discounters reviewed in this chapter first inspect their gowns at their home office before shipping them out to brides. That can add a few extra WEEKS on to the ordering time. A word to the wise: leave plenty of time to order. If the standard bridal shop says you need 12 weeks to order a dress, leave 16 weeks or more if you plan to order online. And then don't forget factoring in time for alterations.

7 **Track all phone calls, promise dates, etc.** Keep detailed records as to who you speak to and when. As mentioned earlier, many of these sites require you to call a phone number or send an email to place an order. Take notes on these conversations. Be meticulous: make sure you note when all balance payments might be due and when the dress should ship. If a deadline slips, don't wait—get on the phone or email immediately to see what's up.

8 No bragging. If you get a great deal online, don't brag about it to the whole world. Major gown manufacturers don't like online gown sellers and might cut them off if they read your post about how much you saved. And don't call up your gown's maker or designer and brag about the killer discount you got. While that may sound obvious, we've actually heard of consumers who did that. Gown makers also monitor wedding chats, newsgroups and other message boards for such information.

The bottom line: ordering a bridal gown or bridesmaids dress online is NOT for everyone. If you don't have time to do extensive shopping or line up a seamstress, it might be more convenient to order in a store.

Another factor: the price of the gown. Think twice about ordering any gown online that retails for less than $500. That's because most discounters will only shave 20% to 25% off the price—hence, the cost of shipping and extras (like steaming or pressing) may come close to outweighing the savings. Gowns over $1000 represent the best online bargains. The savings of shopping online will far outweigh any other costs. Dresses in the $500 to $1000 are a toss-up—price it both in a store and online to make sure you are getting the best deal.

Finally, we should talk about what bridal gown manufacturers think about Internet shopping. Two words: hate it. Dress makers simply despise the idea of brides buying gowns online. Why? They make the majority of their profits from stocking bridal retailers with sample gowns. They fear online bridal shops will cut into their sample profits. As a result, some manufacturers have forced their accounts to sign agreements saying they won't sell on the 'net (those agreements are widely ignored, but are a thorn in the side of online discounters).

That's why we referred to online gown shopping as "not ready for prime time" at the beginning of this section. As long as most online bridal gown sellers are small cottage businesses—and as long as bridal gown makers try to stop it—we won't really see the blossoming of online dress sales. That could change in the future, but for now buying a bridal gown or bridesmaids dress online is for the truly adventurous.

DRESS PICTURE ARCHIVES

Why buy a $5 bridal magazine when you can look at all those dress pictures for free? Plus, add in the power of the Internet to search for just what you want (short sleeves? ball gown? under $800?) and you've got a home run. Here is an overview of the best archives of gown pictures online:

❖ **The Knot's "Bridal Search."** This is The Knot's secret weapon in the wedding web site wars: their incredible dress archive. At last count, they had over 15, 000 pictures online.

You can search by style, designer, price range, neckline or silhouette. We like the fact you can zero in on a gown in your price range—that's one of the big advantages of Bridal Search over a bridal magazine. Simply put, magazines don't print prices (one caveat though: as we mentioned earlier the Knot's price ranges are rather broad). As a result, you can easily fall in love with a gown that is more than a mortgage payment.

So, what's the catch? First, be aware that several of the Knot's designers are very small and obscure. In addition to larger designers, the Knot features small gown makers that sell gowns in, say, four stores. Of course, there's no indication as to whether you are looking at a major player or a small fry.

Our second beef with the Knot: Bridal Search uses bogus style numbers and often has out of date information. The Knot says it simply takes the info it gets from manufacturers and posts it online. That's a cop-out of course. The Knot relies on the traffic of Bridal Search (the manufacturers are not paid for the gown pictures), yet it doesn't seem to do much fact-checking. As a result, you'll see bogus or coded style numbers on the Knot, as well as out of date info on dresses that have long been discontinued.

❖ **Wedding Channel's** (www.weddingchannel.com) "Fashion" section lets you search for gowns, veils/headpieces, accessories and tuxedos. The nifty "Sketchbook Search" lets you zero in on a dress with particular attributes (nine categories—sleeve length, waistline, bodice, etc). Don't know a jewel neckline from a bandeau sleeve? No problem. Just roll your mouse over each word and a cool sketch pops up. Of course, you can just look up dresses by designer, price range and fabric. The Wedding Channel's designer list isn't as extensive as the Knot's, but still includes some heavy hitters (and

Figure 6: Sites like the Knot, Town & Country and the WeddingChannel let you search for the perfect dress by designer, price range, silhouette and more.

fortunately omits quite a few of the Knot's obscure, hard-to-find designers). The biggest disappointment: prices are omitted from some gowns and others have bogus (or missing) style numbers.

❖ **Town & Country Weddings** (http://tncweddings.women. com/tc/) offers a bridal gown search that focuses on upper-end designers like Lazaro and Badgely Mischka ($10,000 bridal gown, anyone?). We found the graphics on this site lacking (the gown pictures looked grainy), but there were at least some prices. So, it's a mixed review for this site. You can see gown pictures from haute couture designers that don't appear on other sites. But the snob appeal (the price ranges *start* at $1000) is a bit much.

❖ **Gown designer web sites.** Yep, most major wedding dress manufacturers have web sites. Some are better than others: the best feature virtual catalogs with high-quality pictures and dress details (fabric, etc.). The worst are one-page affairs with scant links to a few of their retail dealers. The box on page 93 lists web addresses for the biggest gown makers in the U.S. and Canada.

SHAMELESS PLUG AHEAD: BridalGown.com

We'd be remiss if we didn't mention BridalGown.com, a free web site with extensive gown info created by Denise and Alan Fields (yes, the authors of this book). BridalGown.com has all the info you won't get from other wedding web sites or bridal magazines: critical designer reviews, size charts and, best of all, actual dress prices. Read the latest buzz in "Industry News" and check out "Real Brides Say" (stories about dress searches and designers). The "Advice & Tips" section is a free version of our book, *Bridal Gown Guide*. Finally, the site's killer feature: BridalQuote. Submit three dresses to our discount price search engine and we hook you up with dress discounters who bid on your business. And it's all free.

Okay, enough of the shameless promotion. Next up: the best online gown sellers.

Figure 7: Yes, some bridal and bridesmaid designers have helpful web pages. Among the better pages are Mori Lee, Maggie Sottero, Pronovias and Dessy.

GOWN DESIGNER WEB SITE DIRECTORY

Bridal Gown manufacturers

Name	Toll-free	Phone	Web site address
Aleya Bridal		(301) 631-6558	bridaldesign.com
Alfred Angelo	(800) 531-1125	(561) 241-7755	alfredangelo.com
Alfred Sung	(800) 981-5496	(416) 597-0767	alfredsungbridals.com
Alvina Valenta		(212) 354-6798	alvinavalenta.com
Amsale	(800) 765-0170	(212) 971-0170	amsale.com
Bianchi	(800) 669-2346	(781) 391-6111	weddingchannel.com
Bonny		(714) 961-8884	bonny.com
Demetrios/Ilissa		(212) 967-5222	demetriosbride.com
Eden	(800) 828-8831	(626) 358-9281	edenbridals.com
Emme	(888) 745-7560	(281) 634-9225	emmebridal.com
Forever Yours	(800) USA-Bride		foreverbridals.com
Impression	(800) BRIDAL-1	(281) 634-9200	impressionbridal.com
Janell Berte		(717) 291-9894	berte.com
Jasmine	(800) 634-0224	(630) 295-5880	jasminebridal.com
Jessica McClintock	(800) 333-5301	(415) 495-3030	jessicamcclintock.com
Jim Hjelm	(800) 924-6475	(212) 764-6960	jlmcouture.com
Lazaro		(212) 764-5781	lazarobridal.com
Maggie Sottero		(801) 255-3870	maggiesotterobridal.com
Manale		(212) 944-6939	manale.com
Marisa		(212) 944-0022	marisabridals.com
Mary's		(281) 933-9678	marysbridal.com
Mon Cheri		(609) 530-1900	mcbridals.com
Monique	(800) 669-9191	(626) 401-9910	moniquebridal.com
Monique L'Huillier		(323) 838-0100	moniquelhuillier.com
Moonlight	(800) 447-0405	(847) 884-7199	moonlightbridal.com
Mori Lee/Regency		(212) 840-5070	morileeinc.com
Paloma Blanca		(416) 504-4550	palomablanca.com
Priscilla of Boston		(617) 242-2677	priscillaofboston.com
Private Label by G	(800) 858-3338	(562) 531-1116	privatelabelbyg.com
Pronovias	(888) 776-6684	(516) 371-0877	pronovias.com
St. Pucchi		(214) 631-8738	stpucchi.com
Sweetheart	(800) 223-6061	(212) 947-7171	gowns.com
Venus	(800) 648-3687	(626) 285-5796	lotusorient.com

Bridesmaid Manufacturers

Name	Toll-free	Phone	Web site address
Alyce Designs		(847) 966-9200	alycedesigns.com
Bari Jay		(212) 391-1555	bari-jay.com
Belsoie	(800) 634-0224	(630) 295-5880.	belsoie.com
Bill Levkoff	(800) LEV-KOFF	(212) 221-0085	billlevkoff.com
Champagne	(888) 524-2672	(212) 302-9162	champagneformals.com
Dessy Creations	(800) DESSY-11	(212) 354-5808	dessy.com
New Image	(800) 421-IMAGE	(212) 764-0477	newimagebridesmaids.com
Watters and Watters		(972) 960-9884	watters.com, wtoo.com

Note: We left off the "http://www." prefix in front of these addresses for space reasons.

BEST OF THE WEB: DRESSES

With dozens of web sites selling gowns, how can you be assured you are getting a deal and not being taken to the cleaners? First, start with the basics: is the site (or more accurately, the bridal retailer that runs the site) an AUTHORIZED dealer for the gown you want to buy? That is a critical step—some sites that promise big dress discounts buy their gowns from "indirect" sources. Translation: if you have a problem with your gown, the site may have delays in fixing the problem (since they can't go back to the gown's maker directly).

Second, be sure to pay with a credit card. This is a wise strategy for any wedding purchase or deposit. Consumer laws protect payments/deposits made with a credit card; the same protection doesn't apply to checks or cash.

All of these sites discount about 20% to 30% off retail prices you see in stores. Be sure to ask about shipping and any extra fees. Here is our round-up of the best sites to buy gowns online (in alphabetical order):

❖ **BrideSave.com.** Texas-based BrideSave.com offers middle of the road designers like Sweetheart and Mary's. Even though the designer choices are somewhat limited, the site is well designed: search by designer, price range, train, formality, size, skirt, or silhouette. Click on a specific dress and you get all the facts, including online price quotes for specific sizes (a nice touch). You can register with the site to create a "hold rack" of specific dresses so others (friends/family) can peruse your favorites. The site also sells veils/headpieces, flower girl gowns, bridesmaids dresses and accessories—all can be ordered online.

❖ **Gowns Online** (www.gownsonline.com). San Jose-based GownsOnline, an off-shoot of Bay-Area gown seller New Things West, has one of the web's most technologically-advanced gown sites. Click on "Bridal Gowns" and you can search for gowns by price range, dress attribute (train length, silhouette, fabric, waistline, neckline) or designer. Over 3000 gowns are pictured on the site, which is rather impressive. We also liked the cool "Magazine Look-up" feature—pick a bridal magazine, click on a page number and zap! You can see the ad picture, the *real* style number, manufacturer name, retail price and Gownsonline price. Now, that is the power of the web at work.

Of course, there could be some upgrades. GownsOnline's

Figure 9: Most gown-seller web sites are run by local bridal shops. A sampling above includes NetBride.com, GownsOnline, and BrideSave.com.

entry page is an ugly mess—it needs to be improved visually. Finally, the site can run a bit behind with their magazine look-up feature—when we last visited, it looked like they were about two months behind current issues.

But those are minor quibbles: this is still a great site. And here's another hint: GownsOnline is an authorized dealer for many manufacturers that are NOT listed on their web site (thanks to the politics in the industry, designers have requested they not be listed online). Hence it might be worth it to email them for a dress quote, even if you don't see the designer you want listed on the site.

❖ **NetBride** (www.netbride.com) NetBride is a primitive site, but nonetheless has some quite useful information. You can read testimonials about their service, surf gown pictures and read about their shipping policies (included in the price for orders shipped within the U.S.). This site touts their Better Business Bureau ranking, but we'd like to see more information about their parent shop (Rush's of Minneapolis). On the plus side, NetBride has extensive size chart information for major gown makers—that's great. On the down side, we've also noticed the site quotes gowns for lines which they are NOT authorized dealers—that is a big no-no in our book. While we like the fact the site is aggressive on their price quotes, we were a bit put off by that fact. Before you order, confirm that Rush's is an authorized seller for the gown you want.

❖ **Pearlsplace.com** (www.pearlsplace.com) is the online outpost of the Metairie, Louisiana bridal shop of the same name. In business since 1971, Pearl's is owned by Fred and Elaine Schulman. Elaine runs the store (with her daughter Courtney) and Fred is seemingly chained to his computer, running their online operation. Yeah, their web page is a one-page, text-laden affair (you can read which lines they carry, etc.) but Pearl's track record is stellar—they only quote lines they are authorized to carry and ship reliably, say our readers. Best of all, Pearl's carries (and sells online) many of the upper-end designers you won't see at other sites. That said, there are a couple of caveats: first, Fred cannot quote certain designer lines (namely, some of those upper-end gown makers) via email. In those cases, you are instructed to call the store and get a quote over the phone by Elaine. That prospect is hit or miss—when the store is very busy, brides report they are left on hold (a toll call) for a long time or treated brusquely. We wish Pearl's had a dedicated "net guru" at the store who would do nothing but answer the phone from Pearl's web customers.

❖ **RK Bridal** (www.rkbridal.com). This New York City-based retail shop (800-929-9512) has a basic web page with bridal gown and bridesmaid info—you can surf the catalogs of major designers and view individual dresses with style numbers and descriptions (but no prices). Thanks to industry politics, RK requires brides to call their store for a price quote (at least it is a toll-free number). In business since 1985, RK holds forth from a small shop on New York's Upper West Side and generally does a good job at customer service (answering emails and phone calls promptly, etc). They also carry many upper-end brands (not listed on their site) and offer good discounts. Yeah, the site is a bit hokey (how many other gown sites boast a recipes for Noodle Kugel?) but it is worth a visit.

❖ **Romantic Headlines** (www.romanticheadlines.com). The Amazon.com of bridal headpieces and accessories, this site

Figure 9: Romantic Headlines carries just about every headpiece and veil on Earth. We were most impressed with their prices.

features the largest collection of headpieces for sales on the Internet. Dallas-based Romantic Headlines can custom design a headpiece, hat or veil with material to match your bridal gown . . . or you can choose from one of 600 pre-made styles. Want a tiara? They've got 95 pictured. And the prices are excellent. Rhinestone tiaras are $35 to $110, while crystal ones are $70 to $100—that's HALF or more off what most retail stores charge. Regular headpieces with veils are a bargain at about $100. Or add one of their veils (plain or pearl-edged, in a variety of lengths) for just $20 to $60. You can order on-line with a credit card via their secure server and the site also sells bridal accessories, shoes, lingerie, hosiery and jewelry.

DRESS DISCOUNTERS

Some web sites make ordering a gown easier than others. Most do online quotes; others require you to call their store (we note which ones have toll-free numbers). Finally, we look at the price level of gowns they carry. Our comparison:

SITE	EMAIL QUOTES?	TOLL-FREE NUMBER?	STOCK*
BrideSave.com	Yes	No	$
Gownsonline.com	Yes	No	$ to $$
Pearlsplace.com	Yes	No	$ to $$$
RKBridal.com	No	Yes	$ to $$
DiscountBridalService.com	No	Yes	$ to $$
RomanticHeadlines.com**	Yes	Yes	$ to $$$

Key:

Email quotes: Will the site send you a dress quote via email?

Toll-free number: For ordering; most sites suggest you submit questions via email. Discount Bridal Service has a toll-free number (800) 874-8794 for you to find a local dealer; orders are placed through local dealers.

* Stock: What type of stock do the sites offer for sale? $=budget lines ($400-$800 for gowns), $$=mid-price lines ($800 to $1500), $$$=couture lines ($1500+).

** Romantic Headlines sells headpieces and veils, not dresses.

RETAILERS DECLARE WAR ON CYBER GOWN SHOPS

One major gown maker posts a "consumer warning" that ominously warns brides that it "discourages retailers from selling our merchandise over the net." Another group of bridal retailers warns that "chances are the extra charges you will have to pay someone else for fitting, steaming, pressing and shipping will outweigh any (online) discounts."

Yet, books like this say discount gown web sites are a great way to save money. So, what's going on here?

Chalk it up to an old-fashioned range war: cyber stores battling bricks-and-mortar retailers for that elusive bride. In a hotly competitive market, incumbent retailers want to scare the dickens out of consumers, hoping to spook them into dropping any thoughts of online discounts. Anyway, shops say it isn't fair that they stock gowns for consumers to try on, only to have them go online to get a better deal.

We don't buy that argument. Many bridal retailers offer a "one size fits all" model for bridal gowns: full service at full price. Yet, some brides don't want all the service—they just want a rock bottom price. Some brides who buy on the net have never tried on their gown before (albeit a risky proposition since all gown sales are non-returnable, but that's a personal choice). Why should consumers be limited to just one source (that is, bridal retailers) for dresses?

As for the specific allegations that extra charges for alterations, pressing and shipping will outweigh any discount, we have to disagree. First, nearly ALL bricks and mortar bridal retailers charge *extra* for alterations and some even for pressing. Yes, you may have to pay shipping charges, but these are usually minimal (under $20 or $30).

Given the all-out battle over this issue, we do have a couple of suggestions. First, if you decide to order online, be aware the some seamstresses and bridal retailers will try to "punish" you with higher alteration fees (if you come to them for alterations). Hence, it would be wise to NOT disclose to your alteration person where you got the gown (just say you bought it out of town). Some brides have been foolish enough to bring the gown in to a bridal shop for alterations *in the shipping box decorated in big letters with the discounter's name*—suffice it to say, they were not treated well by the retailer.

Coming soon: As we went to press, we understand David's Bridal (www.davidsbridal.com) was preparing to launch an "e-commerce" site. The country's largest chain for off-the-rack bridal shops (over 100 stores and counting) will probably sell a variety of items, including their private-label dresses and accessories. We'll have more updates on David's online efforts and other web sites on our web page at www.CyberBrideBook.com.

FAVORS

Dresses aren't the only thing you can buy online: in fact, they are only the beginning. One popular use for the 'net: favor shopping. These trinkets (given to guests in some parts of the country as a "thank you" from the bride and groom) are perfect for e-commerce. They are small, easy to ship, hard to find in regular stores and often customized. Here's a roundup of places to shop:

❖ **Keepsakes & Promises** (www.weddingfavors.com) is for folks who do NOT want to do-it-yourself—this site sells all sorts of assembled favors in a wide variety of styles.

❖ **Per Favore** (www.perfavore.com) is the home of the "Perfect Favor Maker" and supplies for do-it-youselfers. The site sells precut fabrics, ribbons, bows, do-dads, boxes and printing services. Best part: their "Favor Making University," a free tip archive with tips on making (you guessed it) favors.

❖ **Favorite Things.com** (www.favorite-things.com) is another site with do-it-yourself favor making supplies.

❖ **Favor idea list from Bliss.** (http://www.blissezine.com/library/weddingfavors.asp) Looking for do-it-yourself ideas? This site has six pages of reader-submitted ideas.

❖ **WedNet** has a great list of wedding favor site links (http://www.wednet.com/inspire/favors.asp) that include companies that make candy or chocolate favors to those eco-friendly options like butterflies.

❖ Looking for glass wedding favors? **"A Kiss Glass Sculptures"** (http://www.lymans.com/akiss/) sells engraved glass wedding favors and cake toppers.

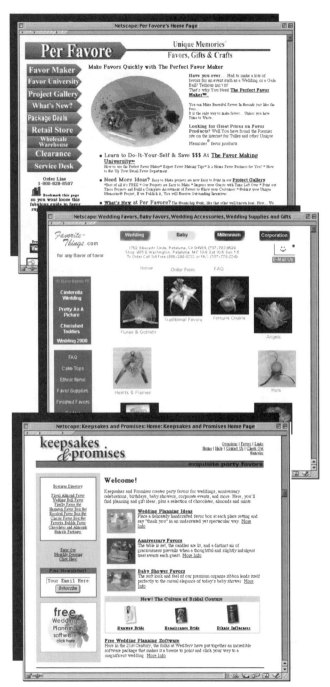

Figure 10: Small companies that make wedding favors can be hard to find—the web evens the odds.

Welcome to the Michaels Arts and Crafts website! Discover ideas, tips, projects, and fun! Find your closest Michaels store and see the Crafts Calendar page for upcoming in-store activities. The Kids Club pages have projects and puzzles. For financial data and shareholder information go to our Corporate pages.

HOME   STORE LOCATOR   CRAFT CALENDAR   PROJECTS   KIDS CLUB   CORPORATE

[**Figure 11: Craft stores like Michaels have web sites with free bridal projects online, complete with instructions and materials lists.**]

❖ **Another idea: craft chains.** The big craft store chains (**Michaels** at www.michaels.com and **Hobby Lobby** at www.hobbylobby.com) each have free "project" areas on their web sites. Search for wedding favors and you'll find detailed instructions and materials lists. Michaels even has a dedicated wedding section at http://www.michaels.com/wedding/index.html.

FLOWERS

Flowers? You can buy flowers over the Internet for your wedding? While that might NOT seem like an obvious e-commerce item for brides and grooms, we've been pleasantly surprised by the emails we get from couples who've gone this route. Here's our top pick for cyber-flowers (reprinted from a review in our book, *Bridal Bargains*):

BEST OF THE WEB

2G ROSES
    Web: www.freshroses.com, (800) 880-0735
    What it is: Flower wholesaler that sells online.
What's Cool: Ever wish you could order flowers at wholesale prices direct from the grower? Thanks to the Internet, you can—2G Roses is our pick as a best buy for brides who want to do

their own flowers. The Watsonville, CA grower has been in business since 1974, but just recently branched out into cyberspace.

Their web site is a floral bargain hunter's paradise. 2G sells much more than roses—you can order lilies, orchids, tulips or hundreds of other available varieties. And the prices? Roses start as little as 50¢ a stem. You can order flowers in individual bunches (say, calla lilies, 10 stems for $10 to $15) or select one of several bridal packages. For example, the "All Rose" wedding features enough roses, greenery and filler flowers to make ten table arrangements, eight boutonnieres, four corsages, four bridesmaids bouquets, one bride's bouquet and a head table arrangement. Price: $340, including shipping (FED-EX overnight to insure freshness).

If that's too much, consider buying a la carte items. For example, enough flowers for a bride's bouquet (25 roses, filler flowers) is just $25 (plus shipping). That might be perfect for a smaller wedding where you just need a bouquet or two. While there is no minimum order, the overnight shipping charges on small orders can be substantial.

Of course, once you get the flowers, you'll need someone to arrange them. If you don't have a friend or relative skilled

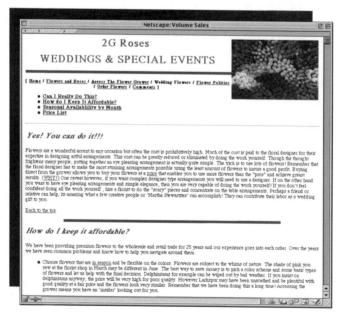

[Figure 12: 2G Roses site won't win any design awards, but they do post prices online and have detailed information about ordering and their services.]

to do that, consider just doing table centerpieces. 2G's "Simple Elegance" package includes enough gardenias, smilax (greenery) and rose petals for 10 table centerpieces. Price: $165, including shipping.

2G's web site clearly explains their packages and how to order, or you can call for a brochure and price list. Most handy was a chart that listed flower availability by month—that way you can tell exactly what blooms are available for, say, an October wedding.

In order to test out this concept, we ordered a sample bunch (25 roses) of mixed color roses from 2G. The short (14" to 18") table roses were $14, with shipping adding another $16 to the tab. 2G sent us an email to confirm our phone order; they were professional and courteous on the phone.

The box arrived on time with an ice pack, bubble wrap and little tags noting the rose names/colors. We should note the roses came tightly budded, with instructions on how to care for them. It took about two to three days for the buds to fully open; unfortunately, four or five roses were duds (they didn't open at all). Nonetheless, we were impressed with the overall quality of the roses, which perfumed our house for quite a few days thereafter.

Of course, 2G Roses isn't the only grower selling flowers at wholesale over the web. Another interesting site is www.flowersales.com, which has extensive price lists on-line that are updated weekly (see the next page for more details). No matter who you order from, consider the following tips:

❖ **Do a small test order first, a few months before your wedding.** That way you can evaluate the flower quality, color and delivery. You can also see how long it takes certain flowers to open. A multi-color bunch is a good idea to see variations in hues.

❖ **Plan in advance.** The flowers may need to arrive a few days before your wedding to insure they open in time. Warm water speeds this process, but it can still take a few days.

❖ **Remember you don't have to go whole hog.** If the thought of doing ALL your weddings via the web is scary, consider doing just the table centerpieces or other decor at the ceremony or reception site. Then hire a professional florist to do the personal flowers (bouquets, corsages, etc.).

FLOWERSALES.COM

Web site: www.flowersales.com

What it is: A flower wholesaler that has extensive links to floral picture web sites.

What's Cool: What's the current wholesale price for tulips? Wonder what those tulip colors really look like? This web site has the answer. We liked the wholesale flower prices, updated weekly for hundreds of flowers from California, Hawaii and Europe. The links on this site (under "Floral Picture Gallery") are fantastic. You can check out the International Floral Picture Database (7000 images, www.floralbase.com), the European Rose Gallery List, the Orchid Photo Page and more. The site also has care and handling tips for cut flowers as well as a list of flowers and their meanings. And, of course, you can also order flowers at wholesale, shipped to you overnight via FED-EX.

Needs Work: The site quotes prices in floral speak, such as Agapanthus for 1.40st (that is, $1.49 per stem) or Feverfew for 4.40bu ($4.40 per bunch). Flowersales.com isn't a pretty site to look at—their main page is just a long list of links to prices, general info and picture galleries. A little more organization would be helpful.

Figure 13: Can't tell the difference between an anthurium and a dendrobium? Flowersales.com has many links to floral picture databases; plus you can see current wholesale flower prices online.

Invitations

Before the Internet, you had two options when it came to ordering wedding invitations: buy in a stationery store or purchase through a mail order catalog. The 'net adds a new spin on that last option: many invitation catalogs now have virtual outposts that let you peruse their offerings without waiting four to six weeks for a printed catalog to arrive in the mail.

Of course, even if you want to go with one of the "prestige" brands sold in fancy stationery stores, the Internet offers some help too: many major invitation printers have web sites that let you view their catalogs online (you are directed to a retailer to order, though). Here's a round-up of what's out there:

Printers

These printers' invitations are mostly sold in retail stationery stores. But some offer online catalogs for you to preview their styles:

Major invitation printers

Name	Toll-free	Phone	Web site address
Carlson Craft	(800) 328-1782		carlsoncraft.com
Crane	(800) 472-7263		crane.com
Embossed Graphics	(800) 362-6773	(630) 236-4001	embossed.com
Encore	(800) 526-0497		encorestudios.com
Regency		(717) 762-7161	regencythermo.com
William Arthur	(800) 985-6581	(207) 985-6581	williamarthur.com

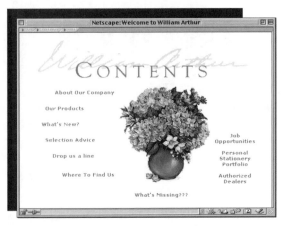

[Figure 14: William Arthur's web site includes excellent advice on selecting invitations. The only bummer: there is no online catalog (just a link to find a local dealer).]

Figure 15: OurBeginning's well-organized site makes shopping and ordering invitations easy.

E-TAILER: INVITATIONS

❖ **OurBeginning.com** (see Figure 15 above) is an online wedding stationery superstore. The company offers hundreds of styles and some interesting interactive features: first you can look up an enlarged picture of any invite. The "Personal Preview" area lets you store invites that you or your friends can look at. Click another button and get an online price quote. Overall, we found this site very well-designed and easy to use. While we didn't have time to do an in-depth analysis of the site's prices, they looked in line with those from mail-order catalogs (the site claims a 20% discount off retail) The only bummer: OurBeginning charges a nominal fee for samples ($2 or so) plus shipping (another $2).

MAIL ORDER INVITATION CATALOGS

❖ **Rexcraft.com.** This is probably the best example of the marriage between the Internet and mail order. Rexcraft, one of the largest mail order invitation catalogs, recently launched this excellent site that lets you view invites, order online, request samples and so on. Pop up screens give you explanations for such optional extras as return address printing and envelope linings.

❖ And more catalogs. **Catalog Orders** (www.catalog.orders. com, see Figure 16 on the next page) lets you order a dozen different invitation catalogs from one site. There are also a few choices for Canadian brides. You can "accumulate" cat-

[Figure 16: Catalog Orders' web site lets you order several wedding invitation catalogs with just one click.]

alogs in a shopping cart and then enter your name and email address one time to have all the catalogs shipped to you. Very convenient.

Do-it-yourself invites

❖ **Formal-Invitations** (www.formal-invitations.com) offers two options: do-it-yourself laser invites and custom printed designs. The do-it-yourself kits let you laser print your text onto translucent vellum (then tie a sheer chiffon ribbon to handmade paper to finish the look). A kit for 10 invitations costs $15.50.

Discount invitation sources

❖ Like the invitations you see in stationery stores but not the prices? **Busy Bride** (www.thebusybride.com) carries 12 top brands, all at a discount of 25% to 35% off retail prices. A reader emailed us with this tip, adding "the service is excellent and fast—I got my complete order in less than a week."

Single-use Cameras

In our *Bridal Bargains* book, we discussed one affordable way of cutting your photography bills: hire a professional to cover the ceremony and then let guests snap away with "single-use" (or disposable) cameras. That way you get the best of both worlds and save money to boot.

But where do you find single-use cameras decorated for a wedding? On the web, of course. We found Wedding Links Galore (www.weddinglinksgalore.com) had three links to sites that sells these cameras:

❖ **The Ultimate Online Wedding Mall** (http://stores.yahoo. com/ultimatewedding/discam.html) has decorated cameras for as low as $5.95 each (for orders of 10 or more).

❖ **C & G Disposable cameras** (www.cngdisposablecamera.com) offers free shipping on their camera orders. Bonus: the site includes a photo gallery of other weddings shot with their cameras to show you the quality of pictures.

❖ **Cameras Unlimited** (www.blarg.net/~camsinc) sells wedding cameras with themes like the Mazel Tov camera.

Figure 17: For some reason, wedding cameras seem to be a popular item to sell online. The Ultimate Online Wedding Mall is a good example.

More stuff to buy online

The online shopping bonanza for weddings doesn't stop with dresses, flowers or cameras. We found virtually every accessory available online as well. Sites like Wednet (www.wednet.com) have online stores that sell wedding bubbles, albums, frames, garters, table centerpieces, gifts, unity candles, cake toppers, books, videos and more. Of course, the Knot.com shills for a similar number of items. While the prices may not be lower than what you'd see in stores, the convenience factor is great (especially for brides who find their time crunched between a job and wedding planning, or for folks who live outside major cities).

Tips & Tricks

As veteran e-shoppers (our credit cards are still smoking from last year's e-Christmas), we have noticed a few tips and tricks to getting the most (and the least hassle) out of shopping online. Our advice:

1 **Always use a credit card.** Consumer protection laws cover payments/deposits made by a credit card—if the online merchant fails to deliver what they promised, you can dispute the charge and get a refund. Pay with a check or cash and you are out of luck if the site disappears.

2 **One word: track.** Keep detailed logs of your e-purchases. That means printing out hard copies of any receipts, confirmation emails, etc. Make sure you write down promised delivery dates. If an item doesn't arrive when promised, don't let a few days or weeks go by—call or email the site immediately.

3 **Be careful of ordering "critical" items online.** For example, if you are a bit timid about ordering online, consider buying just bridesmaids dresses online instead of a bridal gown. If something happens, you can always rush to a department store and get a bridesmaids dress at the last minute. Bridal gowns, however, are more of a "mission critical" item.

4 **Confirm the site is an authorized dealer.** If you are buying invitations online, make sure you are dealing with a site

that is authorized to sell the line. A quick call to a manufacturer or printer's toll-free number may save weeks of heart ache.

5 Beware of the dreaded "backorder." If time is tight, it might be best to call a site and make sure an item is in stock BEFORE ordering it. We've been frustrated with our online shopping experiences by merchants that claim an item is in stock on their web page, only to sheepishly admit later it is back-ordered. While you don't have to confirm the status of everything you order, it might be a good idea for big-ticket items.

FOR BETTER OR WORSE

Shopping online for wedding accessories is really a boon—frankly, it's hard to find this stuff in bricks and mortar stores. Yes, party stores typically stock a few wedding items, but you typically have to live in a big city to get the best deals.

Buying a wedding dress or bridesmaid gown online is a bit tricky: you have to arrange for alterations and deal with mail-order sources long distance. Of course, you must know EXACTLY which dress you want as well, and that can be tricky. Yet, the savings can be very tempting.

Invitations seem like a natural for the web. We expect to see more sites selling invites online, although you still may need to order a sample of the invite to check the paper quality before ordering.

Shopping online may still be in its early stages, but there is one use for the internet that is in full bloom: communicating with other brides, either through chat groups or message boards. We'll discuss that topic in the next chapter.

Community:

Swap stories, ideas and advice with other brides in chats, message boards, newsgroups and more!

Bridezilla. Yep, that's the term the wedding industry slaps on brides who are bit too demanding (albeit behind their backs).

What many bridal merchants forget, however, is how all-encompassing planning a wedding can be. Add the stress of a full-time job and other responsibilities and you can quickly see how planning a wedding can turn normal women into . . . well, bridezillas.

You can witness this obsession first-hand if you attend any of the "bridal shows" that pop up every winter and spring in most cities. For one afternoon, hundreds of brides will cram into a hotel ballroom or convention center to sample cakes, meet vendors and view gowns.

At one bridal show, we met a bride who told us she had already completely planned her wedding. Why would you give up an entire Saturday afternoon to attend a wedding show, we asked her? Her reply was simple: she just wanted to be part of a community of brides. That sounded strange, but as we thought about it, it does make some sense. After all, no one knows what a bride is going through like other brides. Many well-meaning friends and relatives will roll their eyes when you start talking bridesmaid dress colors for the fourteenth time.

But there is good news: today, you don't even have to get

up out of your chair to hang out with other brides, at least in a virtual sense. Chatting with other women planning weddings across the country and around the world is as simple as a click of the mouse. This is one of the Internet's best and most popular features: gathering people together who have similar interests.

This chapter explores all the ways you can use the 'net to join the online bridal community, from message boards to newsgroups and beyond.

How it Works

Internet "communities" for brides come in four flavors: message boards, live chats, mailing lists and newsgroups. Here's a brief overview of each:

1 **Message boards.** Think of these areas as cyber-versions of old-fashioned cork bulletin boards. You post questions and get a reply—or you can merely lurk, checking out other brides' posts. A group of messages under one topic is called a thread. Hence, a single topic area (message board) on a wedding website might have numerous message threads going at one time.

Boards are hosted, maintained and (in some cases) moderated by particular sites. For example, the Knot.com offers a

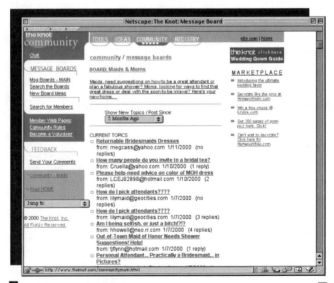

[Figure 1: A sample of The Knot's extensive message boards with various discussion threads.]

whopping 50 message boards on topics ranging from reception ideas to (our personal favorite) "The Bitching Post."

2 **Live chats.** A live chat is like a conference call with potentially thousands of people. Live chats are usually hosted and moderated by the major wedding websites and may address one or many topics. One drawback: conversations on live chats can be somewhat chaotic.

Some live chats are moderated—you submit your question to an online host who relays it to the expert. This helps focus the conversation. Other chats are more free-wheeling. The best thing about chats is the instant gratification—unlike message boards, there is no waiting for a reply. About.com (see Figure 2) hosts a 24-hour a day wedding chat on their site.

3 **Mailing lists.** A mailing list enables the owner of the list to broadcast messages to groups of users via email. When an email is sent to the mailing list name, a copy is forwarded to all the subscribers. There are two kinds of mailing lists: moderated and unmoderated.

[Figure 2: About.com's wedding chat area (http://weddings.about.com/home/weddings/mpchat.htm) is up 24 hours a day, plus features a good FAQ on the topic.]

Real Wedding Tip

Newsgroups

Judging from our reader email, some folks seem to have problems figuring out how to access newsgroups. In the old days, you had to have a separate piece of software (called a news reader) to access newsgroups. Today, all the major browsers (Netscape, Internet Explorer and America On-Line) have built-in news readers. But there is a trick to getting there. In the address or go to line, you don't type http://www., the normal beginning of a web address. Instead, put "news:". For alt.wedding, you enter news:alt.wedding.

As an example, we have a moderated mailing list on our own site at www.bridal-gown.com. Brides subscribe to our newsletter, then we broadcast news and information to those subscribers. On a moderated list, the owner controls what messages go out to users.

On the other hand, an open, unmoderated list lets all members broadcast information to each other and interact without a moderator.

The most popular types of mailings lists are those you can join that are date specific. Let's say you're getting married in August of this year. You can join an August brides' mailing list and hook up with a community of brides all getting married in August. The theory is that you will all be going through similar experiences during your wedding count down and can relate to each other even better than just a group of random brides. (More on subscribing to mailing lists will be discussed later in this chapter.)

4 **Newsgroups.** Similar to message boards, these are not moderated or owned by a particular web site. In fact, newsgroups are a separate part of the Internet (away from the World Wide Web) in an area called the

Usenet. Technically known as online discussion groups, thousands of newsgroups cover every conceivable interest. The two major wedding newsgroups are news:alt.wedding and news:soc.couples.wedding (see the real wedding tip on the previous page for more now to access the newsgroups).

In order to post questions to a newsgroup or view a newsgroup discussion, you have to have "news reader" software. The good news is that the three major browsers (Netscape, AOL and Internet Explorer) have already incorporated news readers into their software.

Figure 3: What the newsgroup alt.wedding looks like when you open it in a Netscape browser.

The top pane lists message threads or topics (including when they were posted).

The bottom pane lets you view individual messages. The original message is often shown in italics, with the response below.

REALITY CHECK

Now that everyone and their third cousin has an Internet account, the web isn't exactly a cozy place for conversation. The sheer size of many message boards, chat rooms and newsgroups makes the conversation like that in an overcrowded coffee house—the cacophony of it all can overwhelm any usefulness.

Many sites listed in this chapter can have literally hundreds of new posts daily with little or no organization. You could find yourself sifting through all that to pull out only tiny nuggets of information. Separating out the banal conversation from the truly useful stuff is not easy.

When it comes to mailing lists, beware of email overload—some active lists send out some 200 emails EACH DAY. We're not sure how anyone reads that many posts, let alone gleans anything useful unless they have a black belt in speed reading.

Another reality check to these bridal "communities:" flame wars. Some chat areas or message boards have members who endlessly bicker or insult each other over trivial topics. Yes, moderators are often available to curb flaming, but it can pop up without warning and take some time to banish offenders from the list.

The bottom line: 'net boards, chats, newsgroups and the like are fun to play with, but are more like meringue than filling. The amount of fluff here often exceeds the substance.

THE BIG SEVEN

If there's anything the Big Seven do well, it's bringing large numbers of brides together. Here's an overview

❖ **The Knot** (www.theknot.com) has 50 plus message boards (click on Message Boards on main screen) divided up into seven well organized categories: Getting Started, Wedding Ideas, Fashion & Beauty, Knot Newlyweds, Gift Giving and Vendor Listings. Getting Started lets you hook up with other brides by month or geographical location. Wedding Ideas includes topics like Big Day on a Little Budget and Destination Weddings. Finally, the Hot Topics area includes the Bitching Post, Sex & Romance and other spicy topics.

Live chats are available throughout the day starting at 11 am Eastern time and going virtually every hour until 10 PM. They even have a daily newlywed chat for folks who can't tear themselves away from the Knot even after their wedding is accomplished. Each chat is moderated by a host to focus the discussion.

❖ **Bliss** (www.blissezine.com) offers a wide variety of message boards, some moderated, some not. Three moderated "Ask the Experts" forums include "Wed"iquette (see a review in the next chapter), Floral Frenzy and the Next Step Dance.

Unmoderated forums include topics such as Jewelry, Budgeting and Ethnic Wedding. They also offer regional forums, allowing you to chat with brides in your state and city. When we last visited the regional sites looked a bit empty, however.

Chat rooms are also available on Bliss' site organized into topics like General, Bridal Showers, Beauty and Health, Grooms, Honeymoon/Destination Weddings, Newlyweds, Religious Wedding Customs and 2nd Time Brides. Perhaps the best (and we bet the most popular) chat topic is the Vent chat. Chat rooms are open 24 hours a day, but they also have suggested meeting times to spur group interest.

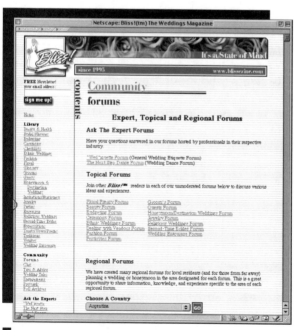

Figure 4: Bliss offers a dozen forums, including regional message boards.

❖ **Todaysbride** (www.todaysbride.com) does offer a "Bride Talk!" section on their site with a general chat area. The only topic we could find on our visit was simply a general "make new friends" chat. They do allow you to see postings for up to the last year in case you want to sift through recent conversations.

❖ **Modernbride.com** (www.modernbride.com) not only hosts chats on line (bringing in famous bridal designers for marquee value) but keeps transcripts of past chats online in case you missed out. Their events are actually Yahoo! Chats, so they can be accessed through www.yahoo.com as well.

❖ **Wedding Channel** is oddly devoid of chat groups and message boards. The site seems to put more emphasis into articles and advice, which will be discussed in the next chapter.

Red Flags

While you may find the community aspect of the World Wide Web intriguing, useful, even entertaining, there are some potential problems lurking out there in the ether. For example, in most cases, you'll have to register to join chats and message boards. Giving up your email address may invite an inordinate amount of spam (junk mail). Make no mistake, web sites love selling your email address and personal information to advertisers—be sure to check the site's privacy policy to see how the site will handle your info.

One way to beat the spam is to set up a separate email box to post to message boards, newsgroups and mailing lists. See Tips and Tricks later in this chapter for more details.

Be sure to avoid filling out lots of personal info. For example, one site, ModernBride.com, asks you to register before you can participate in their chats or message boards. Besides the usual user name and email address, their server eShare asks for phone number, snail mail address, even hobbies (see Figure 5 on the next page).

Be wary also of revealing too much in your conversations on line. We've seen numerous brides slip amazing details about themselves into postings on line. Avoid giving out your snail mail address, wedding date, and other personal facts. You may even want to use another name when you're out surfing these message boards, chats and newsgroups.

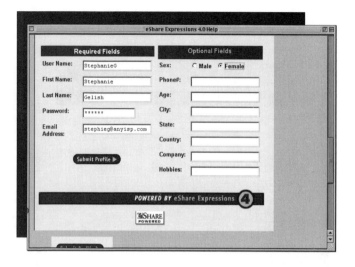

Figure 5: Many web sites ask you to register before you can access chat or message boards. Sometimes the questions get a bit personal. ModernBride's sign-in area is above, including such optional fields as your age, phone and hobbies.

BEST OF THE WEB

ULTIMATEWEDDING.COM'S WEDDING CHAT
Web Address: www.ultimatewedding.com or www.weddingchat.com

What It Is: Ultimatewedding.com hosts some terrific community pages on their web site offering a discussion board, live chat room, and mailing lists (by date or topic). See Figure 6 on the next page.

What's Cool: The site's subscribable mailing list topics are pretty extensive including Weddings and Kids, Jewish Weddings, Canadian Weddings and more. Ultimate Weddings' message boards address wedding planning (including etiquette), life around the wedding (career and family issues), brides by month, and geographic groups. All this is free, of course ... but the best news is the site does NOT require you to give up any personal information to register. You can also keep your screen name hidden for additional privacy.

Needs Work: The site's sign in screen can be a bit intimidating, asking for your ICQ address and specifying certain signature formats, without really explaining what these things are.

Figure 6: Ultimate Wedding's "community" area includes access to their message boards, including a listing of recent discussion items.

YAHOO CLUBS

Web Address: http://clubs.yahoo.com then search for wedding to find all the wedding-related clubs

What It Is: An incredible number of clubs founded by individuals on the most diverse topics imaginable.

What's Cool: Anyone can start a club on Yahoo! These clubs are all unmoderated and can focus on any topic under the sun. We saw clubs titled Young Adult Love and Weddings, On Line Wedding Consultant and, our personal favorite, the Greek Polish Wedding Club (focusing on New York and New Jersey Greek and Polish weddings). Over 50 clubs were online when we last visited. Don't see one you like? Yahoo lets you create your own for free, with option of restricting access to just your friends.

The only downside to Yahoo's bridal clubs: some can be rather lonely. A random check of a couple dozen sites revealed less than ten members in most cases.

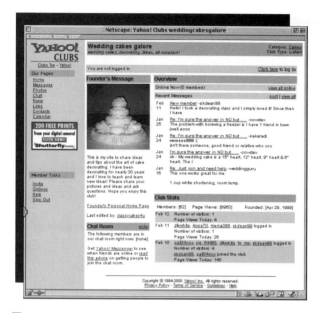

Figure 7: A taste of Yahoo's wedding clubs: this one focuses on wedding cakes.

DELPHI WEDDING CHATS AND MESSAGE BOARDS

Web Address: http://forums.delphi.com then keyword search for wedding

What It Is: Delphi is a site devoted solely to forums and message boards. The topics available are amazingly diverse.

What's Cool: We found wedding related sites like the Disney Wedding Bulletin Board, Las Vegas Brides and much more. Delphi seems to attract non-traditional brides to their sites and will even allow you to create your own forum. While you have to register with the site if you want to participate in the chats, we like how you can lurk in the forums without registering if you just want to check it out.

Needs Work: The first thing to hit you when you open Delphi's forum site is the clutter. We're talking BIG time clutter here—just navigating this site takes some patience. A few of the forums (including the Canadian wedding forum, for some reason) are in unbelievably small type that's hard to read. Also, on our visit, the search function wasn't working so we had to sift through the entire Lifestyles section to find all the wedding sites. (See Figure 8 on the next page).

[Figure 8: Delphi's site has an amazing number of
wedding-related forums, but the site is rather
cluttered and hard to navigate.]

Another Site to Consider

❖ **Town & Country** magazine has its own site at www.
tncwedding.com with access to Women.com's wedding bulletin boards. We found eight topic areas aimed at brides and
noted a lot of action on the boards. The site offers etiquette
advice, fashion forums and planning advice as well as other
topics. Joining Women.com is free and quite simple (very little personal information required.)

Tips and Tricks

❖ To avoid a massive advertising blitz when you sign up for all
these great chats and message boards, consider setting up a separate email box. There are several free email services on the web
that make this easy. A good example is Microsoft's **Hotmail**
(www.hotmail.com), but you can also find free email at
Yahoo.com and Lycos.com. We like Hotmail best—the coolest feature to this site is the ability to read your Hotmail from Microsoft's
Outlook Express email client. Or view it anywhere from a web

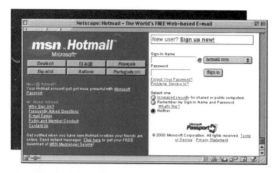

Figure 9: Microsoft's free Hotmail let's you set up a
separate email box for all your bridal-related email.

browser. Directing all your "bridal" email makes it easy to separate
this from your personal or work emails; plus it keeps spam and
other unwanted junk out of the rest of your accounts.

❖ Many web sites are confusing to navigate. Just finding the
chats and message board locations can be a challenge. Quick
tip: look for the keyword "Community." This seems to be the
universal web term that applies to chats and message boards.

❖ If you want to chat, go for prime time. Chat rooms can be
very lonely when you don't visit during "prime time." Most
chat rooms are busiest during the lunch hour or in the
evening after 7 PM Eastern time. Some sites even offer a listing of their most popular times for chatting. Another tip: look
for special events to get the most out of chat experiences.

For Better or Worse

If your friends, relatives and fiancé are downright
sick of your constant talk of weddings, where can
you turn? The Internet is a great place to vent, share
ideas and just plain talk with other brides. The best part: you
can gab on to your hearts content on topics large (his parents
hate you and don't want to come to the wedding) and small
(should you register for a set of crystal liqueur glasses?). All
this is available 24 hours a day, seven days of week.

The downside: there's nothing like bitching to a friend in
person. And the Internet is loaded with folks who know it all—
and don't mind telling you about it. Take any advice you receive
online with a grain of salt. And perhaps an aspirin or two.

Advice:

Got etiquette

questions?

Need advice

on planning?

Use these

sites to find

the answers.

You don't plan a formal party for 200 of your closest friends and relatives every day, so it's no surprise that weddings bring up lots of questions. What is the proper way to do *this*? Is this the correct way to do *that*?

And heaven forbid, if you happen to do THAT at your wedding none of your friends will ever speak to you again, right?

Prior to the Internet, wedding etiquette could be summed up in two words: Emily Post. Her book, first published in the Jurassic period, has succeeded over the years in providing a road map for engaged couples to follow.

As in many parts of society, however, technology seems to be outpacing the efforts of etiquette gurus to come up with new rules. For example, should you allow an online bridal registry to email your gift list to your wedding guests? Is that a great convenience for guests . . . or a tacky faux-pas that makes you look like a doofus.

The web can be a good source for wedding etiquette, as well as advice on questions to ask vendors, bridal shower ideas and more. In this chapter, explore which sites have the best up to date trends and ideas.

How it Works

Etiquette on the Internet is generally available in three varieties: Frequently Asked Questions (FAQs), article archives and newsgroups.

1 Frequently Asked Questions (FAQs). FAQ's are generally a beginner's guide of the most often-asked etiquette questions. These might include topics such as how to deal with divorced parents or how to *not* invite small children to your wedding. Let's face it—the questions you have are probably the same ones others have been asking for years. If you have a question that isn't included in their FAQ, some sites have a direct email link you can use to ask a specific question of an etiquette expert.

2 Article Archives. Other sites often include archives, with brief articles organized by topic area. If you're looking for tips on hosting a bridesmaids luncheon or questions to ask a tuxedo shop, this is the place to go.

3 Newgroups and Bulletin Boards. Finally, the newsgroups mentioned earlier in Chapter 7 can be helpful. Here you'll find all the free advice you can imagine from brides going through exactly the same experiences you are.

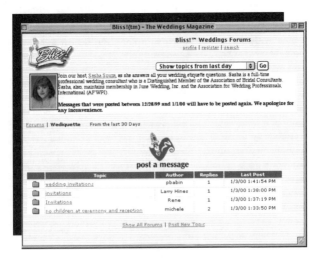

[Figure 1: Bliss (www.blissezine.com) offers an etiquette forum where users can post questions that are answered by the site's advice expert.]

REALITY CHECK

While the Internet can potentially link you with hundreds or thousands of sources for friendly advice and etiquette, there are some downsides to the extended web community:

❖ **Unqualified advice.** Be careful who you get your etiquette from. Miss Manners and (other etiquette authors) have been studying and writing about etiquette for decades and can truly be characterized as experts. But beware of just any yahoo who puts up a web page and starts offering advice. One etiquette "expert" advised a bride who didn't want children at her wedding to simply put "Adults Only" on her invitation—that's clearly a 15 yard penalty for unnecessary tackiness.

❖ **Self-serving tips.** Some advice is put up by vendors trying to sell you things. A great example: web sites run by formal wear manufacturers that recommend you put "Black Tie Invited" on all wedding invitations. Gee, we wonder who would benefit from that recommendation? Wedding gown manufacturers have been known to put out a "consumer warning" on their site trying to keep brides from ordering their dresses from online discounters. This isn't done to protect consumers, but rather to placate full price retailers. (Where do you think the online dress discounters get their dresses? The same gown designers who rail against the 'net on their sites. Most quietly sell to 'net sites on a hush-hush basis).

❖ **Advertorials.** Many of the Big Seven web sites will have unlabeled advertorials within their advice section. An "advertorial" is basically advertising masquerading as an objective piece of editorial advice. Frequently, you'll find an article on one of the major wedding web sites that rambles on about, say, a honeymoon destination—including a mention of a resort with a convenient link to the resort's home page. Is there any labeling of such paid-for plugs as advertising? Don't bet on it. While we understand the need for sites to make money from advertising, we think full disclosure would help boost their credibility.

WISH LIST

Etiquette sites on the web are like a lake that's a mile wide, but only an inch deep. Simply put, depth is lacking. On one site, we saw a section devoted to adding "African American Traditions" to weddings. The subsequent article had two measly suggestions for doing this. How helpful is that?

We'd also love to see more about regional trends and practices. For example, you won't see any mention of the custom among Hispanics in the Southwestern U.S. to have sponsors pay for various parts of the wedding and reception. Ditto for Southern traditions like having the father as your best man in the Carolinas. Many big sites pay short shrift to the bridal customs of Asian communities as well.

THE BIG SEVEN

Some of the Big Seven web sites started out as online bridal magazines—so you might expect them to be brimming with advice. In some cases, that's true. Here's the lowdown:

❖ **The Knot.** (www.theknot.com) Check out the "Ideas" section for some interesting "real world articles" from couples describing their own weddings. You can read about ocean side nuptials in Maine or elaborate weddings in Texas. Best of all, the articles have pictures and in-depth descriptions of how couples pulled off various events. We've got to hand it to the Knot—the site's articles cover everything from "customs and traditions" to "cultural and ethnic ideas," "interfaith issues" and beyond. You even can read articles on remarriage, destination weddings, same-sex unions, vows and readings. The only negative: some of the articles are a bit dated (we noticed a wedding story from 1994).

❖ **The Wedding Channel**, (www.weddingchannel.com, go to the "Planning" button). Wedding expert and accessories maven Beverly Clark offers very general etiquette advice and wedding planning tips. Beyond Beverly, there are tons of articles with advice and ideas ranging from "What's Hot in Wedding Favors" to "Planning the Bachelorette Party." Our biggest beef with this site is its lack of organization. You'll have to look through the entire list to find an interesting

Figure 2: A sampling of the advice sections at the Knot, Modern Bride and the WeddingChannel.

topic. It would help if they would index the articles more clearly. The best part of this site is their "real bride" stories, discussed later in this chapter in the Best of the Web.

❖ While we like **Bliss'** (www.blissezine.com) "Wed"iquette Forum, the wedding expert who answers some questions failed our "no kids at the wedding" test. She recommended putting "Adult Reception Following" on your invitations—a big etiquette no-no. Bliss' community bulletin boards were good places to find tips and advice and the site's archives featured numerous past articles on traditions as well.

❖ **Modern Bride** (www.modernbride.com) has its own "Planning Potpourri" with a plethora of advice on etiquette and planning. Much of the content felt like it had been transplanted directly from the magazine—that works for some articles, but other pieces lacked the "pithy" quotient that works better on the web than in print.

❖ **Weddingbells.com** (www.weddingbells.com) shines when it comes to bridal advice. Their comprehensive section includes areas titled "Ideas," "Planning and Etiquette," and "Trends and Traditions" section.

Figure 3: Weddingbells.com's "Ideas" section features color pictures to illustrate their suggestions such as a unique cake topper (the cheese is made of marzipan).

Ideas/Inspirations is devoted to helping make your wedding unique. Yeah, some of these ideas sounded hokey to us, but it can't hurt to browse the 150-odd ideas. The "Gallery of Inspirations" includes nifty photos that offer still more ideas such as cake toppers or table setting suggestions (see figure 3 on the previous page).

The "Planning" section features an excellent question-and-answer area, while "Trends & Traditions" tackled cultural and other ethnic trends.

BEST OF THE WEB

CRANE'S ONLINE WEDDING BLUE BOOK

Web Address: www.crane.com/wedding_blue_book.html or www.crane.com (then click on social stationary and then on etiquette).

What it is: The best place to find the most consistent answers to your invitation etiquette questions. Crane also explains the "anatomy" of your typical wedding invite.

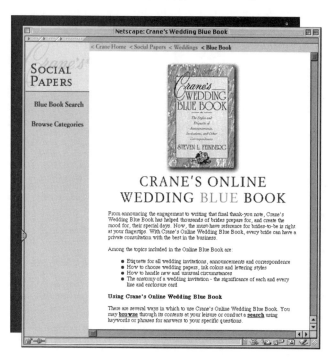

Figure 4: Crane's online Blue Book of etiquette is the bible on invitation wording and addressing.

What's Cool: Crane practically invented the modern wedding invitation, so they know just about everything there is to know about addressing and wording them. Based on their Crane's Wedding Blue Book tome (available for sale on the site), the online guide allows you to browse their expert advice or launch a targeted search to help you solve your invitations quandaries. We browsed through the wedding invitations section, clicking on the "Divorced Parents" sub-topic. We were impressed with their clear, concise advice about the correct wording in a variety of sticky situations.

You can also see samples of invitations for Mormon weddings, Hispanic weddings, even double weddings. Crane explains different traditions and give information on the use of various invitation enclosures. This should be required reading for brides before they go shopping for invitations.

Needs Work: The search function on this site disappointed us; we couldn't find any info on topics that we thought were obvious. The browse function seems to be the best bet to find information. We also wish Crane's no-nonsense information could be expanded to other etiquette issues besides invitations. We found their presentation refreshing compared to other "chatty" etiquette sites.

WEDNET'S ENGAGING QUESTIONS AND LIBRARY

Web Address: www.wednet.com/questions/ default.asp or go to www.wednet.com and click on "Engaging Questions" or "Library"

What it is: One of the best etiquette FAQ's with detailed, accurate information.

What's Cool: This site is easy-to-use with simple search functions. The "Engaging Questions" page is divided into categories and includes answers to questions about family difficulties, clothing and beauty, and even theme weddings. We like the tone of the "experts" and found their answers thoughtful and helpful. WedNet's "Library" is a compendium of articles on various planning aspects of a wedding. A quick search for info on "wedding cakes" turned up nine articles, from how to cut a cake to preserving your cake. The search options seem endless with hundreds of articles available.

Needs Work: This may be a minor quibble, but we couldn't find a way to send the site's etiquette experts a question. Isn't "interactivity" what is supposed to make the web so cool? Yea, there is a general email address, but no direct email link.

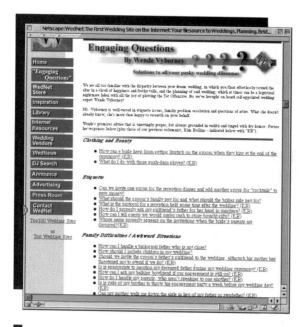

Engaging Questions
By Wende Vyborney

Solutions to all your pesky wedding dilemmas

[The navigation sidebar reads: Home, "Engaging Questions", WedNet Store, Inspiration, Library, Internet Resources, Wedding Vendors, WedNews, DJ Search, Announce, Advertising, Press Room, Contact WedNet, Top100 Wedding Sites or Top Wedding Sites]

[Figure 5: WedNet's "Engaging Questions" focuses on wedding etiquette questions and answers.]

OTHER SITES OF INTEREST:

❖ The **WeddingChannel** (www.weddingchannel.com, click on the Bride button to find these articles) features stories from "real brides" in three categories: Bride's Diary, Featured Bride and A Bride Looks Back.

As it sounds, the Bride's Diary is a periodic update of the trials and tribulations a bride goes through when planning her wedding. The Featured Bride is actually a couple who shares their plans for their wedding day. And A Bride Looks Back focuses on the 20/20 hindsight all folks have on nuptials after the big day has come and gone.

While we think this section is well-written, we have to wonder if the advice is too general to be of any specific help to other brides and grooms. On the upside: the site regularly updates this section, so you can check back for new installments.

❖ **Etiquette Hell** (www.thinds.com/jmh/ehell/index.htm) is a fun web site chock full of amazing etiquette mistakes, tacky wedding stories and funny bridal faux pas. We were mesmer-

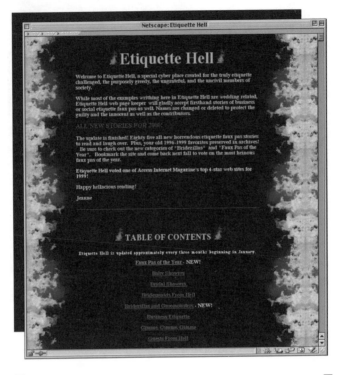

[Figure 3: Etiquette Hell's offers a bit of comic relief by providing a forum for etiquette horror stories.]

ized by this site, which is sort of the cyber equivalent of stopping at the scene of a car accident on the highway. Our favorite story: the exotic dancer bride who stripped at her own wedding. Other topics included Bridezilla and Groomonsters, Bridal Showers, Bridesmaids from Hell, even Tacky Wedding Vendors.

For Better or Worse

Is the web any better than going to the library and checking out Emily Post? Maybe, maybe not. The problem with web site etiquette is the time it takes to find the info. You'll do a lot of hunting and pecking before you'll find the answer you're looking for—if you can find it. You may even have to wait for an answer from a web site's "expert." In many cases it may be easier to head to the library, check out a book and look up the topic in the index.

ETIQUETTE SPOT CHECK

How well do the wedding etiquette sites answer basic questions? We looked up the answer this perennially thorny one: what if you don't want any children at your wedding? Here are the responses and our take on their answers:

SITE	ANSWER	OUR TURN
The Knot	Tell friends & family; address invites to adults	Good response
Wedding Channel	Address invites to adults	Appropriate
Bliss	Put "adults only" on reception card	Tacky, tacky
Wed Net	Ducks issue— no advice	The easy way out?
Modern Bride	Call first to give parents a head-up event will be adults-only	Not bad

Yeah, it seems old-fashioned, but it is effective. Of course, in this busy world, etiquette changes faster than Miss Manners can type her column (and technology is often responsible for the changes). Certainly the web can adapt as quickly, while books take much more time to update.

While wedding etiquette help on the web can be spotty, there is one use for the Internet that has great advantages: the bridal gift registry. We'll discuss this topic in the next chapter.

Register:

Tips & tricks to using online bridal registries

Ever since the words "e-commerce" entered the lexicon of shoppers and Wall Street traders, bridal registries have been the Holy Grail of the digital retail world.

And a quick look at the numbers reveals the story: the wedding gift registry biz racks up some $17 BILLION in sales each year. With 29 million net users buying something online in 1999 (up from 19 million in 1998), the time seems right to marry the old-fashioned gift registry with the Internet. It seems an easy step to link up a retailer or department store's gift registry (which in most cases are already computerized) to the Internet so your Aunt Mabel can buy that perfect place setting from the comfort of her living room 1000 miles away from the store, right?

Well, not so fast. We found many online gift registries were long on hype and short on delivery in the real world. In this chapter, we'll try to separate the winners from the losers in the online gift registry race.

How it works

Online gift registries work the same way as the offline versions: you go to a store and register for which gifts you want. The online registries add another twist: some let you register for gifts online—no store visit necessary. (See the chart below.)

Guests can either buy gifts in stores or (and this is where the web-heads start to salivate) online. A few clicks and a gift is purchased and whisked to you via the mail. Theoretically, your registry is instantly updated to reflect purchases. And you can change your registry online, adding items, changing quantities and the like.

So, how do online registry sites make money? Basically, most get a cut of each sale from the department store or other retailers. One site, the Knot, actually sells their own slew of gift items and fulfills orders from their own warehouses.

Reality Check

Notice we used the word "theoretically" in the above how it works section. The reality of online registries is not as pretty. Some drawbacks:

❖ **Version 1.0.** Even though the Internet has been in full bloom since the mid 1990's, online gift registries only took off

Who's Zooming Who?

Just keeping track of who is affiliated with whom on bridal registries is a never-ending task. Here is the latest list:

Gift Registry Site	Affiliates
Della.com	Crate & Barrel, Neiman Marcus, Restoration Hardware, REI, Gumps, Sharper Image, local store.
Modern Bride/ Wedding Network	Bed Bath & Beyond, Sur La Table, Smith & Hawken, Ross Simons.
TheKnot.com	None (the Knot sells its own products).
WeddingChannel	Macy's, Bon Marche, Burdines, Goldsmiths's, Lazarus, Rich's, Sterns.

in 1998 and 1999. That's because many of the department stores were hesitant at first to give a chunk of their revenues to "partners" with dot-com in their names. That changed in early 1999 when Federated Department stores invested millions in WeddingChannel.com to become their online registry partner and Della.com received more millions from venture capitalists. The upshot: every store big and small has rushed to the web, dragging their gift registries behind them.

The problem: many of these services still have a "Version 1.0" feel to them—glitches, goofs and outright screw-ups have dogged these sites in the past year. Sure, with the millions of investment capital flowing into these sites, you get the feeling they will fix the rough edges. But when? Will online registries be ready for prime time in 2000? Or will we have to wait until 2005? Or 2010?

❖ **Over-promise, under perform.** Online gift registries wow brides with the promise of all sorts of techno-wizardry. Wouldn't it be cool to get an email letting you know a guest purchased a gift the moment it happened? That way you could get a head start on all those thank you notes and maybe even adjust your registry to add in new items if needed.

The email feature was a big promise of Della.com, one of the registries we'll review later in this chapter. Yet, a Wall Street Journal reporter who tested this service found it lacking—despite numerous purchases, there were no emails. Della claims this glitch happened because the items were back-ordered or the retailers didn't notify Della of the purchases yet. (The reporter's advice: check the site instead of relying on email notifications).

Another bummer: Della.com promised brides they could register at local stores and have those items listed online. The reporter for the Journal spent several hours at Gumps picking out crystal and china, only to later discover that all her guests could view or buy online from that store were gift certificates. Della.com promises the local store gift option will be online sometime in mid 2000. But why did the site promise that in the first place before it was ready to deliver?

❖ **Shiny new service, same old problems.** Just because your bridal registry is on the Internet doesn't eliminate many of the problems that have dogged bridal registries for years. We hear numerous complaints from brides and grooms about gift registries from both big department stores and small retailers.

Examples: items that are backordered for weeks, duplicate gifts, problems with returns, sale prices that weren't honored and more. Just a warning: fasten your seat belts, because using a bridal gift registry can be a bumpy ride.

WISH LIST

Is it too much to ask that a bridal registry would work as promised? That is, you register for items, guests buy them and they get marked off your registry. While that doesn't seem like a big request, many large department stores can't seem to figure out even the fundamentals of this business.

Adding the Internet and all its promises of interactivity to registries sounds like a great idea. But if the big boys can't even get the basics right, all the fancy 'net technology in the world doesn't matter.

THE BIG SEVEN

Sometime in 1998, most of the Big Seven web sites came to a realization that online advertising sales alone weren't enough to sustain their operations. Many turned to e-commerce as a cure-all for their cash flows—and online registries were one of the hot new trends.

[Figure 1: The Knot has its own in-house registry with name brands but no retail store partners.]

Interestingly, the Big Seven have taken varying approaches to gift registries. Some have partnered with big department stores; others have decided to go it alone, building their own in-house registries. Here's an overview:

❖ **The Knot** (www.theknot.com) has taken a strange path in the online registry world. Instead of partnering with a department store or other retail chain, the Knot decided to go it alone, building its own in-house registry. (See Figure 1 on the previous page).

Unlike other web sites that allow you to register at retail stores, the Knot requires brides to register online. Guests must also purchase their gifts online as well.

The Knot offers 10,000 products from 500 name brands in the registry. Besides traditional china and crystal, the Knot also offers outdoor gear, entertainment and travel gifts. You can even register for mortgage payments, car loans or mutual funds.

Like all online registries, you can modify and monitor the registry at any time. The Knot also lets you specify delivery dates and offers instant messaging and toll-free phone customer service.

Instant Messaging

Some sites (like the Knot) offer Instant Messaging services to help with your registry questions. But what is Instant Messaging? This is a small piece of software that sits on your desktop and lets you "instant message" friends, family or anyone else with the same software.

The biggest providers of Instant Message software are America Online (www.aol.com) and Microsoft (www.msn.com). The software is free and you don't have to have AOL or MSN as your internet service provider to use it.

On the downside, we were put off by how difficult it was to use the site. A quick video about the registry tells you nothing; you have to register to get any info on how this works. By the time you get to choose products, you are left adrift in categories with as many as 100 items to choose from.

The Knot tries to make the registry more interactive by suggesting gifts for various lifestyles (adventure, romantic, cosmopolitan are the choices, believe it or not). Behind the scenes, the Knot's partner QVC provides all the warehousing, sales, fulfillment and distribution with the Knot registry.

We're not sure if the Knot has taken the correct path here. The limits of the Knot's approach to online registries are obvious—guests who don't have online access must call a toll-free number to order gifts. That doesn't sound very convenient to us. There is no touching or feeling the merchandise for either the guest or couple.

❖ **The Wedding Channel.** This site has partnered with Federated Department stores (Macy's, Bon Marche, Burdines, Goldsmith's, Lazarus, Rich's and Stern's) to do their online gift registry.

[Figure 2: The Wedding Channel's registry is linked to Federated Department stores like Macy's.]

First, you must create an "Our Wedding" account with the site. Then you pre-register on a "profile" form where you fill out your name, address, wedding details, and which store you want to register with. Then a real human calls you to set up an appointment with their "partner store" near your home.

The key advantage to this is that you get to actually see the items you are registering for. And guests can purchase online, in the store or via an 800-number. Of course, you get the same interactive features as other registries: you can view and modify the registry online.

The Wedding Channel has taken a high-tech approach to its registry. In 1999, the site tested a program with kitchenware retailer Sur La Table that installed kiosks in their stores with Internet access. To register, couples used a Palm Pilot computer to scan items and returned the handheld computer to a cradle to upload the info to Wedding Network's registry.

The disadvantages to the Wedding Channel's registry? First, if you don't have a Federated-brand department store near you, then that's just tough. You're basically left to the same online options as the Knot (creating an online registry; having guests buy online, etc). The delivery times on some items can be long (one glass decanter was 16-18 weeks). And the Wedding Channel doesn't have any "non-traditional" stores in its registry besides the standard china, crystal and kitchen gadget categories.

And, as we've complained before with other parts of this site, the Wedding Channel's registry is pretty to look at but rather pathetic when it comes to explaining how it works. There is a "planner" section with articles on what a kitchen appliance is (doh!) but the site really needs an interactive tour or explanation of how the registry works.

❖ **Modern Bride.** This site has partnered with the Wedding Network, which has Bed Bath & Beyond, Sur La Table, Smith & Hawken and Ross Simmons (among two dozen other stores) as part of their registry. This site does have some non-traditional categories like home furnishings, "outdoor lifestyles" and more. One nice feature: the site offers optional password protection to limit access to your registry to just guests and family. (See Figure 3 on the next page).

❖ **Today's Bride** (www.todaysbride.com) offers a low-tech bridal registry. You can create a list on the site with what you want and which stores carry that gift. When you receive a

Figure 3: The Wedding Network's online gift registry is plugged into retailers like Bed, Bath & Beyond and Ross-Simons.

gift, you are supposed to go to the site and check that item off your registry. We were underwhelmed with this site—what's the point of creating this list?

❖ **Other sites.** Bliss simply refers users to the Wedding Network, while WedNet has partnered with Della.com (see below). Wedding Bells doesn't have any registry partner at all.

BEST OF THE WEB

DELLA.COM
Web: www.della.com or www.dellaweddings.com
What it is: The largest online wedding gift registry.
What's Cool: Despite its teething troubles (see earlier in this chapter for details), we have to give Della the award for the best wedding gift registry. Hands down, this site has the most going for it.

Della (formerly called Della & James) was founded in 1998 and got its name from the O'Henry short story "The Gift of the Magi." (The characters Della and James in the story gave up their most prized possessions to buy gifts for each other).

Della has an impressive group of backers that have pumped $45 million into launching the site, including

Amazon.com, Neiman Marcus, Crate & Barrel and Williams Sonoma. All in all, the site has 30 stores with their registries online, including Dillards, REI, Restoration Hardware, Gumps, Sharper Image and more. Even better, Della has local stores in a limited number of cities (Boston, Chicago, Dallas, Los Angeles, New York, San Francisco and Seattle) online as well.

You can register one of two ways: in the store or online (at least with some stores). Della has an excellent series of tools in case you need help, including a product guide, checklist and even an interactive "consultant." The latter asks you about your lifestyle, cooking needs, how you spend your weekends and other issues before recommending several items.

Like all online registries, you can view and modify your registry online. The site lets you track which gifts are sent and (allegedly) emails you when guests make purchases. The prices are the same at Della as in the store; the site also promises to honor all sale prices.

Needs work. We've already knocked Della for their problems earlier in this chapter. See the "Reality Check" for details.

Beyond those problems, we still don't like the "announce"

[
Figure 4: Della has the most partners for its site, including such stores as Dillards, Neiman Marcus and Crate & Barrel.
]

feature of sites like Della. The company promises to "tasteful-ly inform your guests about your registry or wedding page through our complimentary guest notification service. We'll help you keep your friends and family up-to-date on your plans." Translation: Della will send your guests an email pitching them to buy gifts. Sorry, that's just plain tacky.

❖ **Other gift sites.** You don't have to register with a "wed-ding" site for your gift registry. Several other interesting web sites are also vying for this market.

Among the most interesting: **Ewish** (www.ewish.com), a general gift registry with partners such as Pier 1, JCPenney, Ross Simmons and Amazon.com. You can enter a "wish list" of needed items or register with one of their partners (guests can view your registry in a "framed" window direct-ly from Ewish).

WishClick (www.wishclick.com) lets you add any item to your wish list while you shop at such sites as Crutchfield, Ebags, Proflowers.com and other sites. This site is very well-organized with excellent FAQ's (frequently asked questions).

The Gift.com (www.thegift.com) has a search engine that lets you locate gift choices (such as items under $20). Their affiliates include Black & Decker, Panasonic and others. You can just look up gift ideas or create a registry (my.gift.com).

Some retailers have gone their own way with gift reg-istries. Among the best of the retail sites: **Williams–Sonoma** (www.williams-sonoma.com). Their excellent site lets you cre-ate or update a gift registry, select gifts, get ideas and more.

And it's not just the big boys—smaller discounters have gotten into the online registry act as well. **Michael Round**, a DC-area discounter of tableware and other kitchen items has a web site at www.mround.com. You can look up reg-istries online, order gifts or just learn more about the store. The company offers a 25% discount off retail and has a toll-free number (800) 467-6863 for guests who don't live in the DC area.

Have an experience with an online gift registry you'd like to share? We'd like to hear from you: contact us at authors@CyberBrideBook.com. Or call (303) 442-8792.

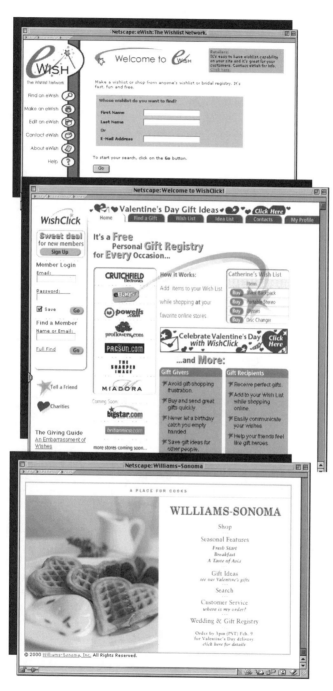

Figure 5: A selection of other gift registry sites, including Ewish, WishClick and Williams-Sonoma.

Tips & Tricks

1 Don't register too far in advance. Online registries urge you to register AS SOON AS POSSIBLE! But do you really need to? First, guests don't buy gifts nine months before your wedding. Second, if you register too early, there is a chance that some items in your registry will be discontinued, back-ordered or sold out. The best advice: register two or three months before the wedding.

2 Confirm return policies. If you register online, go to the site's policies page and print out their return and exchange policies. If there is any dispute, you will have a written record to refer to.

3 More registry tips. We found a great web site with consumer tips on bridal registries: www.BridalTips.com (there's a link to their advice on registries on the main page). The authors are consumer advocates with solid advice and tips. You can read about the Place Setting Price Game, phantom sales and other problems with registries. (The specific address with the registry advice article is: www.bridaltips.com/registry.htm).

[Figure 6: BridalTips.com includes some good tips on avoiding gift registry scams.]

For better or worse

Are online gift registries better than the way it used to be? The answer is clearly yes—the ability to view/modify your registry online is a killer feature. And the convenience for guests (at least those that are wired) can't be beat.

In our opinion, the best online registries are those that combine the best of both worlds—bricks and mortar (picking out gifts in person at a store; letting guests buy in a store if they wish) and the Internet.

We're less sure of the net-only options like the Knot. Doing all your gift business online has drawbacks. Returns is a biggie: the logistics of returning wrong gifts is troublesome (packing, costs, etc). Not being able to see and touch those expensive items is another major negative.

Of course, it's up to brides and grooms (and their guests) to decide which approach to the gift registry will work. We have a hunch that the general concept of the online gift registry is here to stay.

GROOMS:

Hey you! Wake up! Yes there are web sites out there for guys!

Yes, we realize this book is called "CyberBride." But, that doesn't mean there isn't something for the groom to do on the web.

Granted, there aren't as many sites out there for grooms as there are for brides (okay, we found just a handful). And most of the major web sites just have token "grooms" sections that are little more than a few tux pictures and a couple of articles on proposals.

But, we didn't let that deter us. Here are some of our favorite grooms' sites.

THE BIG SEVEN

We found better grooms' advice on other web sites (see later in this chapter), but the Big Seven do have a few interesting morsels:

❖ The **Knot's** Grooms and Guys channel features articles on decorating the getaway car and grooms duties (22 to do's). You can read topics like "garter toss basics" and "first dance do's and don't's." Other topic areas touch on "groom grooming," bachelor parties and guy gifts. The Knot's Tux Glossary is good, but the site show's its bride bias here—there is no tux picture gallery like the Knot's 10,000+ bridal gown picture archive.

Netscape: WeddingChannel.com - Fashion Search

WeddingChannel.com

LOG IN   SITE INDEX

| Bride | Groom | Guest | Our Wedding | Fashion | Shopping | Registry | Planning | Travel |

tuxedos & suits   WeddingChannel.com
click here ... we can help

FASHION HOME
FASHION SEARCH
gowns & dresses
veils & headpieces
accessories
tuxedos & suits

DESIGNER LIST
GLOSSARY
ARTICLES

Raffinati - Cambridge

TUXEDOS & SUITS

Select your criteria (we recommend no more than 3 choices), then click 'SEARCH' below.

Any Designer
Any Color
WC#:   SEARCH
Style #/Name: CLEAR FORM

Jacket
○ Cutaway
○ Dinner
○ Double Breasted
○ Mandarin
○ Suits
○ Tailcoat
○ Other

Vest
○ Backless
○ Fullback
○ Waistcoat

Buttons
○ Single
○ 2 Button
○ 3 Button
○ 4 Button
○ 5 Button
○ 6 Button (Dbl. Breast)

Lapel
○ Notch
○ Shawl
○ Peak
○ Mandarin

Shirts
○ Band
○ Mandarin
○ Turndown
○ Wing

Slacks
○ Flat Front
○ Pleated
○ Stovepipe/Baggy

SEARCH
CLEAR FORM

[Figure 1: Looking for a cutaway jacket with shawl collar? The Wedding Channel's tux search will find it.]

❖ **The WeddingChannel.com** does a better job with tux pictures—the site posts a searchable tux index. Pick a designer, color and style and the site will give you some possibilities. Other groom areas here feature diamond choosing advice, groom's gifts and proposal do's and don't's.

BEST OF THE WEB

UNGROOM'D
Web: www.ungroomed.com
What it is: A man's twist on weddings & matrimony.
What's cool: Yes, it is the first and probably the best site for grooms and grooms-to-be. Draped in manly black graphics, the main page leads you to articles on typical groom topics (diamond buying, popping the question), but there are some quirky items. Example: The Ungroom'd Police Blotter, with stories about terrible things that happened to married folks.

Ungroom'd does hawk merchandise, as most sites do. Their "GroomRoom" includes a large selection of groomsmens' gifts (cigars, barware, jewelry, electronics, sports gear,

Figure 2: It's manly but I like it too! Read about Jerry Seinfeld's wedding at Ungroom'd, a "men's perspective on marriage."

etc). The site does run periodic sales (we noticed a 20% off deal on a recent visit).

Coming soon: unButtoned, a promised area with formal-wear tips and advice.

Ring Advice

Got to buy wedding rings? A diamond engagement ring? The web offers some decent advice. Some possible sites:

❖ **Wedding Ring Hotline** (www.weddingringhotline.com) is a source we first wrote about in our *Bridal Bargains* book. This company offers great deals on all manner of wedding and engagement rings. Their online outpost includes a virtual catalog, a price list, detailed ordering information and more.

❖ **Diamond Cutters** (www.diamondcutters.com) has a good

tutorial on buying a diamond. We also liked Diamond Cutters International's "tricks of the trade area" (www.diamondcuttersintl.com, go to the articles section). Each includes scams and rip-offs to avoid when looking for a ring.

❖ **About.com**'s Wedding section features a five-page guide to buying diamonds. We thought the advice was solid and on target. (http://weddings.about.com/home/weddings/library/weekly/aa121099a.htm)

❖ **Diamond Grading** (www.diamondgrading.com/) is jam-packed with diamond advice. We liked the extensive FAQ's on diamond buying, including a glossary, appraisals services, a chat group and more.

❖ The newsgroup **Soc.Couples.Weddings** offers a great FAQ on diamond buying at www.wam.umd.edu/~sek/wedding/mlynek.html

❖ **5c Diamonds** (www.5cdiamonds.com) is another diamond seller with an extensive buyer's guide online.

TUXES

Gingiss (www.gingiss.com) has tuxedo style gallery with a couple dozen tux pictures, plus a question-and-answer section on "appropriate styles," "what the groom should know" and more.

4Tuxedoes (www.4tuxedoes.com) has numerous links to companies that both sell and rent tuxedo, plus a Q&A on tuxes and more.

eTuxedo (www.etuxedo.com) claims they are the largest discount retailer of tuxedos. Prices start at $169 for a wool tuxedo. The site includes a history of tuxedos and answers to fashion questions.

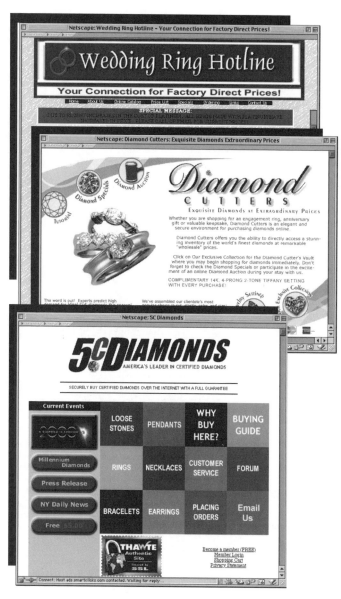

Figure 3: Ring and diamond buying advice from the Wedding Ring Hotline, Diamond Cutters, and 5C Diamonds.

Honeymoon:

Travel sites have boomed on the 'net. But where are the best deals? We found 'em.

While many wedding web sites might still be in there "formative" stage, travel sites are in full bloom on the 'net.

Hard to believe, but it was not so many years ago that if you wanted to get airfare prices, tickets or hotel accommodations for a honeymoon, you basically had one source: the travel agent. Or you could sit on the phone on hold trying to reach an airline or hotel reservation line.

Today, all this and more is on the 'net. You can book airfares, car rentals and hotel rooms with just one click.

Does that mean travel agents are obsolete? Of course not. A good agent may still have first-hand knowledge of resorts and other tricks of the trade. Yes, many agents now charge fees to cover their services, but you may want to compare the prices. Even after booking fees, a travel agent may find a better deal, especially on package tours.

Here's our list of the top ten things you can do on the Internet to book your honeymoon:

1 **Jump on low fares.** Airfares change every hour and sometimes every minute as airlines try to squeeze every last dollar out of travelers. Beat them at their own game by surfing Best Fares' free "Newsdesk" (www.bestfares.com).

We have found this resource to be the best at tracking fare sales and other short lived deals (the site calls them "Snooze Alarm" deals, as in "these fares are so short lived, if you snooze you lose them"). When we last visited, we saw fares to Europe for as little as $150, a Waikiki hotel for $99 a night and numerous other deals.

You don't book travel directly on this site; just use the information to jump to airlines, hotels or other travel sites to book the special deals. We've found the information to be very credible and timely.

The downside? All the deals are arranged chronologically (not by city or destination), so you have a lot of scrolling to do. There is no search function, leaving users to just sift through all the deals one at a time. Also, some of the deals are for Best Fares members only ($60 annual fee). But we've found enough deals in the public or non-member side that you don't need to subscribe.

The specific address for the newsdesk at Best Fares is: http://www.bestfares.com/travel_center/desks/newsdesk.asp

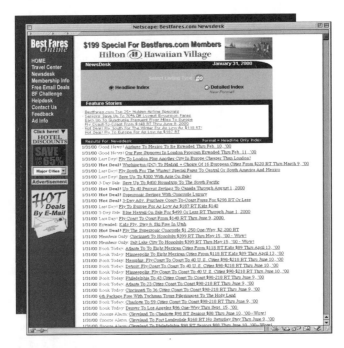

2 **Take an e-fare honeymoon.** An empty airline seat or hotel room is a perishable commodity—it can't be resold later and is money down the drain for travel companies. Hence, airlines, hotels and car rental companies try to dump excess inventory during their special e-fare sales.

Here's how they work: every Wednesday, the airlines (and others) post special deals on their web site. Travel must start the following Saturday with a return on Monday or Tuesday. These are the slowest travel days for airlines (since business travelers don't fly then) and hence the airlines, hotels and car rental companies try to fill seats/rooms/cars.

You can't beat the deals: Chicago to Miami for $169, anyone? The same weekend we saw Dallas to San Francisco for $189. Hotel rooms at fancy resorts can often be had for $75 to $150 a night (basically, half-price) and car rental deals abound as well. There are also international e-fares that have longer travel periods and other special deals from tour companies.

The downside? You won't know where you'll go on your honeymoon until just three days before (so it helps to be adventurous). The deals vary from week to week; you never know what city will come up.

How to find the deals? Yes, you can find these specials on each airline, car rental or hotel site—but that takes a lot of surfing. A better bet: try a web site like Last Minute Travel (www.lastminutetravel.com) which tracks all the deals. Another source: Best Fares newsdesk (mentioned above) posts HUGE charts every Wednesday that categorize all the deals for airlines, hotels and car rentals.

3 **Track specific fares with email alerts.** You've zeroed in on a particular honeymoon destination, but the airfares are sky-high? Wouldn't it be great to get an email when the airfares go on sale?

Travelocity.com (www.travelocity.com) offers an excellent free service called Personal Fare Watcher. Select any five city-pairs and the web site automatically gives you the lowest fare out there. And here's the cool part: if the fare dips or rises more than $25, the site will automatically email you to tell you the old and new fares. We've found some great fare sales this way.

Another neat feature: if you select that low fare, Travelocity gives you a calendar to select departure and return dates. You can instantly see when a fare is available (some have restrictions that you have to fly certain days of the week, etc.). The site also warns you if certain days are already sold out.

The only bummer: the sale fares sometimes have so many restrictions (such as holiday fares) they are hard to take advantage of. But if you remain flexible with your travel plans, you can get some great savings.

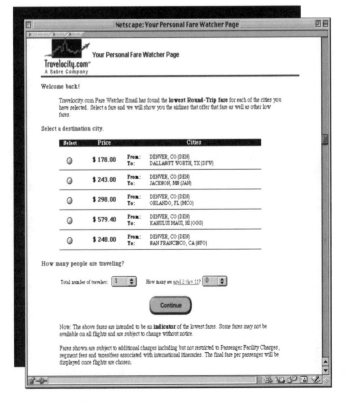

4 **Bid on a honeymoon with an auction site.** Don't like the prices you get from a web site or travel agent? What if you could name your price for airlines, hotels, car rentals and more?

Priceline.com is one of the 'net's most popular travel sites thanks to their "name your own price" service for travel. In recent months, Priceline has added more airlines to their mix, making it more convenient for travelers.

So, how does it work? You tell Priceline when (a date) and where you want to travel and the price you want to pay. They search for deals that match that price. (How do they do it? Airlines and other travel companies can dump their inventory of unsold seats on this site without sparking major fare wares. Priceline keeps the difference between what you bid and what they pay for tickets).

The downside? You have to enter a credit card BEFORE you know whether your bid is accepted. Another major bummer: Priceline often will book you to travel at funky times (you don't have a choice when you fly). Most tickets will have connections (instead of non-stop flights) and that can lead to delays if bad weather follows you on your honeymoon.

One tip to using Priceline: check a "general" web site like Microsoft's Expedia (www.expedia.com) to get an idea of what the "going rate" is for airfares, hotels, and car rentals you want. Then bid under those amounts. (As a side note, Expedia also has an auction site called "Flight Price Matcher" that is similar to Priceline). Other travel auction sites include Bid4Travel.com and DriveBudget.com.

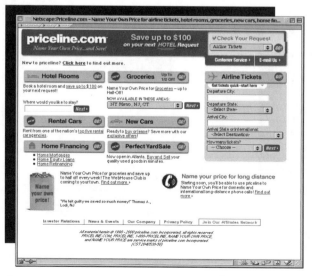

5 **Get the best hotel deals.** The Hotel Reservations Network (www.180096hotel.com, another Best Fares-related web site) offers some great deals on hotels both here and abroad. You do have to pay for these deals in advance with a credit card (and you can't cancel), but the deals might be worth it. Another source for discount hotel rates: QuickBook.com, which doesn't require pre-payments.

Once you find hotel rates on this site, put down the computer mouse and pick up the phone. That's because the best deals for lodging are often found by calling the hotel directly. Ask if they are having any specials, discounts (like AAA) you might be eligible for and more. Generally, we've found these rates to be lower than what you find on the web.

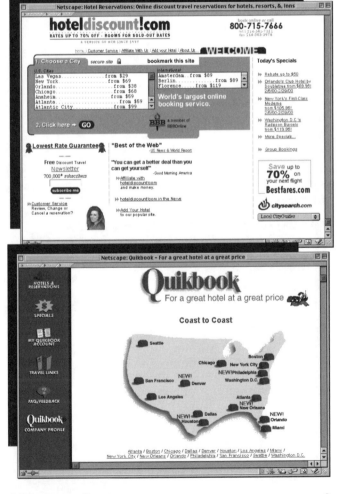

6 **Check out LowestFare.com.** This web site has a secret weapon: Carl Icahn. The former owner of TWA struck an unusual deal with the airline in 1995 that gives him the right to buy an unlimited quantity of tickets from TWA at 45% off published fares. Icahn sells these tickets at LowestFare.com, which works much like other travel web sites (you enter when and where you want to go and the site retrieves fares). The only catch: travel cannot begin or end in St. Louis and you almost always have to change planes in St. Louis. Yet, the deals are very good: we priced a Denver to Orlando trip during Spring Break week at just $273 through this site; other sites were charging as much as $500 for these dates.

7 **Hit the consolidators.** These companies buy large blocks
of tickets from airlines and then sell them to the public at
discounted prices. A good example is 1travel (www.onetravel.com), which offers some good bargains (especially on international flights).

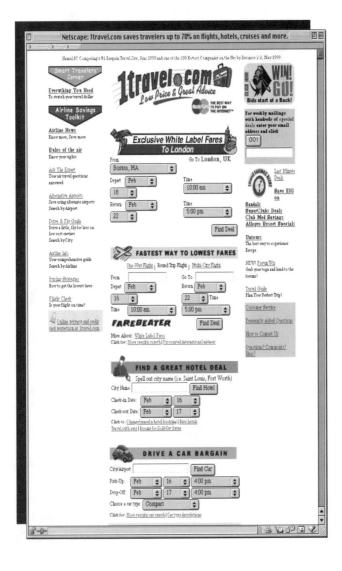

8 **Check out the tour companies.** Tour package operations like Sun Trips (www.suntrips.com) and Apple Vacations (www.applevacations.com) sell tour packages that combine airfare and hotel rooms at rock-bottom prices.

The cool part: since they specialize in vacations, destinations include such popular spots as Hawaii, the Caribbean and Mexico. The deals are generally better than what you would get if you booked with an airline and hotel company separately.

The downside: Tour companies typically use charter airlines (not major airlines) to get you there. And sometimes your flight options will leave or arrive at odd times (5am departure anyone?). On the upside, most flights are direct or have at most one stop (you don't have to fight with any connections).

Another bummer: as of this writing, most tour companies require you to book through a travel agent, although we suspect Internet booking may not be far down the line.

9 **Consider a destination wedding.** Why not forget this entire wedding thing and get married where you'll have your honeymoon? This is an especially attractive option for second weddings, when you've already done the big white dress and fancy party thing.

Destination Weddings & Honeymoon magazine has an entire web site devoted to this concept at www.dwh-magazine.com. You can read articles about different destinations and the logistics of getting married there. The magazine also recently launched a web site called Wedding Trips (www.weddingtrips.com) that will actually book travel shortly (call 877-WED-AWAY for more details).

Many cruise lines also offer wedding packages—check those specific sites for details.

10 **Two words: Microsoft Expedia.** There are many travel web sites out there, but we have to give it to Bill Gates. His Expedia site (www.Expedia.com) is really the best. We love the ease with which you can look up and book airfares, hotels, car rentals and more. Expedia's travel articles are also well-researched articles and cover many destinations and honeymoon possibilities.

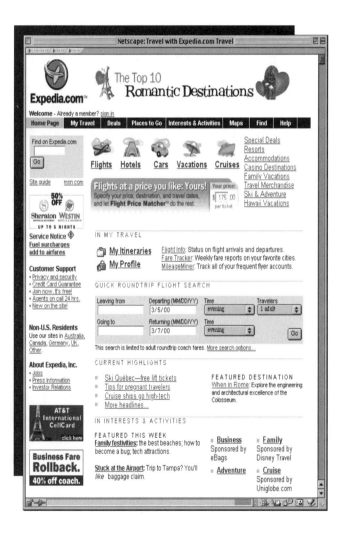

Conclusion:

So, what's the bottom line with the Internet and weddings? Are we better off with this thing or what?

Even the most ardent Luddite would have to admit the World Wide Web has transformed many aspects of life—planning a wedding included. We've seen first hand how competition from web-based discounters has lowered bridal gown prices. And with Wall Street showering millions in venture capital dollars on wedding web sites and 'net gift registries, you get the feeling the fun is just beginning.

Yet, the Internet isn't a cure-all for all your planning woes. There are still many aspects of getting married that have to be done the old-fashioned way—visiting face-to-face with merchants, negotiating deals, and buying products. And our cynical antennae always shoot straight out when we hear a new web site hype their "cool feature" ... when we find that it works ONLY on alternate Tuesdays when the moon is full.

The bottom line: it is darn tricky forecasting the future of technology and tying the knot. Okay, maybe there won't be holograms standing in for the out of town guests as we speculated in this book's introduction. But you can't watch all the 'net hysteria and not wonder how things may change in a few years. Could anyone have guessed the future of air travel after watching Orville and Wilbur Wright's first wobbly efforts at Kitty Hawk? Or predicted the future impact of television by watching "Your Show of Shows?"

So, we'll end this book by acknowledging this story is just beginning. We'll try to stay on top of the crazy world of bridal web sites, both here in print and on our web site, www.CyberBrideBook.com. Stay tuned.

Appendix:

Power 'net tips: make your email wireless, super- charge your browser and more.

Okay, you're an official web-head. You're addicted to the Internet, spending hours surfing for the latest travel tidbits on Mozambique honeymoons.

Alright, maybe you haven't gone that far, but there are several ways to supercharge your web surfing. Here are our tips for power 'net brides.

1 Make your email wireless. Yea, the web is the sexy part of the Internet, but email is the workhorse. Once you go email, it's hard to ever go back. With more and more bridal merchants wired into email, you may find yourself using this tool to send a quick message to your florist, caterer or dress shop.

The big problem with email: it's usually chained to your desktop computer at work or home. Well, we've been testing a new system that makes your email wireless: Elink, by American Mobile.

Elink uses a small, pager-like device (see Figure 1, the Elink web site on the next page) that works like, well, a pager. It pulls your email off the Internet and sends you the messages on the device, which is made in Canada by Research in Motion.

The best thing about Elink: you use your own email address (any POP3 account will work; the device can't retrieve AOL mail, however). Elink leaves a copy of

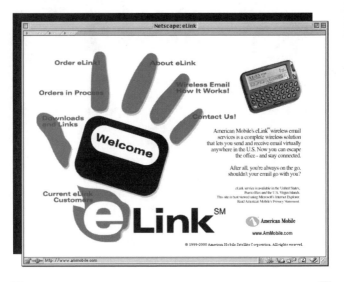

Figure 2: Elink offers a small pager-like device to make your email wireless.

your email messages on your mail server and lets you sync your messages and address book (Windows only).

(A small technical note: Elink actually offers two services: Elink Agent and Elink Messenger. Elink Agent lets you use your existing email account. Elink Messenger sets up a separate email address. In our opinion, Elink Agent is the best way to go).

Even though the Elink device is small, it's very easy to use. You basically use your thumbs to type out quick emails. A thumb-wheel acts like a mouse, enabling you to scroll across the screen.

We've used a demo unit of Elink for the last few weeks and have been impressed. The screen is bright and includes a back light. Since it works on a pager network, you can send or receive messages in just about any city or town. And the battery (one AA) lasts for three or four days even with heavy usage.

The only downside: Elink offers no Mac-sync software, so we couldn't import our email addresses to the unit. And sometimes Elink dropped emails (we got a "truncated" error message) where we could see the email subject and sender, but no message. (But that was only in less than 1 in 100 messages.)

Elink has two costs: one for the pager ($350 or so) and the other for service. The company offers a limited service plan for $25 (you are limited to 24,000 characters per month) or unlimited service for $60. Yea, that's pricey but if you are a heavy email addict, you'll find it worth it.

2 Open multiple windows at once. Browsers like Netscape and Internet Explorer can often chew gum and walk at the same time. Hence a good tip to speed up your web surfing: open up several windows at once. You can load in several sites at once. Another idea: when you see a link at a site you'd like to jump to, hold down your mouse button to select "New Window with this Link." That way the new site opens in a new window and you can surf the existing site while the new one comes in the background.

3 Customize your browser. We're amazed at the number of folks who never tweak the "preferences" files of their browsers. Both Netscape and Microsoft offer impressive customization features for users, if anyone is paying attention. If you have a slow 'net connection, for example, you can turn off the pictures and keep them from loading at each site. That will make things seem downright zippy by comparison.

4 Kill the fancy stuff. Turn off all the graphics and Java features in your browser. Yeah, those animations and scrolling graphics are cool, but they slow everything DOWN to a crawl on most dial-up connections. (Once again, look at the Preferences section of your browser to turn off all these features).

5 Keep the plug-ins under control. There is no limit to the creativity of web site developers who INSIST you must have this cool new plug-in to enjoy their site. We say: keep it simple. The only plug-ins you really need are Real Audio (www.realaudio.com) and Macromedia's Shockwave (www.macromedia.com). Another useful extra: a PDF (portable document file) viewer like Adobe's Acrobat (www.adobe.com). Technically, Acrobat isn't really a plug-in since you can launch it as a separate application.

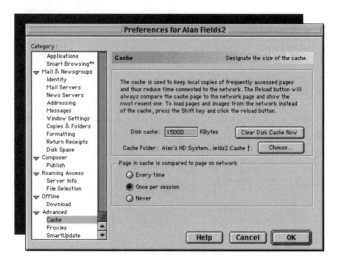

[Figure 2: Boosting your cache (adjust the setting in this preference menu) can speed up surfing.]

6 **Boost the cache.** Most computers come with gigabyte hard drives—put that space to use by boosting the cache levels in your browser (cache levels can be changed in the preferences section of your browser, see the above figure). Double your cache and see what it does to speed your surfing.

7 **Tame your bookmarks.** Yes, it is easy to just add to your bookmark section when you happen on a cool wedding web site—until your bookmark list looks like War and Peace. Take the time organize your bookmarks into folders (dresses, flowers, planning, fun stuff, etc). (Okay, we don't follow our own advice on this one, so please don't look at our bookmark list. But that doesn't mean you can't keep things tidy).

WEB SITE DIRECTORY

Wonder where these contact names appear in the book? Check the index later in this section for a page number. Refer to the chapter in which they are mentioned to see which companies offer a consumer catalog, sell to the public, etc. For space reasons, we omitted the "www." prefix in front of the web site addresses.

Contact Name	Web Site

Chapter 1 Intro

Authors, Alan & Denise Fields	CyberBrideBook.com

Chapter 2: The Big Seven

Bliss	blissezine.com
The Knot	theknot.com
Modern Bride	modernbride.com
Today's Bride	todaysbride.com
Weddings Bells	weddingbells.com
Wedding Channel	weddingchannel.com
WedNet	wednet.com
IBride	ibride.com
Martha Stewart	marthastewart.com/weddings/
USABride.com	USABride.com
Wedding Network	weddingnetwork.com

Chapter 3: Plan

Modernbride's interactive calendar	
	modernbride.com /weddingplanning/calendar_frame.cfm
Knot's Big Day Budgeter	theknot.com/budgetermain.cgi
Knot's Ultimate Wedding Checklist	theknot.com/ checklist.cgi
Knot's The Guest List Manager	theknot.com/guestmanagerintro.cgi
WedServ	Wedserv.com
HudsonValleyWeddings	
	http://hudsonvalleyweddings.com/guide/budget.htm
Weddingshowroom.	
	weddingshowroom.com/weddingshowroom/budget.html
Wedding Solutions	wedding.co.za/9806/articles/WBudgets.htm
1800Wedding.com	1800Wedding.com
When.com	when.com

Wedding Planning Software

Bride's Mate	http://bridesmate.com/.
I Thee Web	itheeweb.com
My Wedding Companion	fivestarsoftware.com
Wedding Concierge	weddingconcierge.com
Wedding Magic	bridalink.com/store2/magic.htm

Chapter 4: Create

Web Sites

Ecircles	ecircles.com
Homestead	homestead.com
Wedding Web Sites	wedding-websites.com
The Wedding Day	theweddingday.net
Ultimate Wedding.com	ultimatewedding.com/webring.htm

Invitations

Wedding Invitation Kit	pcpapers.com
Bridal Crafts	
BridalCrafts magazine	bridalcrafts.com

Chapter 5: Find

Great Bridal Expo	greatbridalexpo.com
Digitalcities.com	Digitalcities.com
Excite's travel pages	excite.com/travel.
Timeout.com	Timeout.com
USA Citylink	usacitylink.com
Yahoo's city guide	http://local.yahoo.com

Professional Associations

The Professional Association of Custom Clothiers	http://paccprofessionals.org
The National Association of Catering Executives	nace.net
Wedding and Event Videographers Associations	weva.com
June Wedding (wedding consultants association)	junewedding.com
The Professional Photographer Association	ppa.com

Weddinglinksgalore.com	Weddinglinksgalore.com
Smartbride.com	Smartbride.com
Here Comes the Guide	herecomestheguide.com

Chapter 6: Shop
ShindigZ   shindigZ.com

Dresses
Bridal Gown manufacturers

Name	Toll-free	Phone	Web site address
Aleya Bridal		(301) 631-6558	bridaldesign.com
Alfred Angelo	(800) 531-1125	(561) 241-7755	alfredangelo.com
Alfred Sung	(800) 981-5496	(416) 597-0767	alfredsungbridals.com
Alvina Valenta		(212) 354-6798	alvinavalenta.com
Amsale	(800) 765-0170	(212) 971-0170	amsale.com
Bianchi	(800) 669-2346	(781) 391-6111	weddingchannel.com
Bonny		(714) 961-8884	bonny.com
Demetrios/Ilissa		(212) 967-5222	demetriosbride.com
Eden	(800) 828-8831	(626) 358-9281	edenbridals.com
Emme	(888) 745-7560	(281) 634-9225	emmebridal.com
Forever Yours	(800) USA-Bride		foreverbridals.com
Impression	(800) BRIDAL-1	(281) 634-9200	impressionbridal.com
Janell Berte		(717) 291-9894	berte.com
Jasmine	(800) 634-0224	(630) 295-5880	jasminebridal.com
Jessica McClintock	(800) 333-5301	(415) 495-3030	jessicamcclintock.com
Jim Hjelm	(800) 924-6475	(212) 764-6960	jlmcouture.com
Lazaro		(212) 764-5781	lazarobridal.com
Maggie Sottero		(801) 255-3870	maggiesotterobridal.com
Manale		(212) 944-6939	manale.com
Marisa		(212) 944-0022	marisabridals.com
Mary's		(281) 933-9678	marysbridal.com
Mon Cheri		(609) 530-1900	mcbridals.com
Monique	(800) 669-9191	(626) 401-9910	moniquebridal.com
Monique L'Huillier		(323) 838-0100	moniquelhuillier.com
Moonlight	(800) 447-0405	(847) 884-7199	moonlightbridal.com
Mori Lee/Regency		(212) 840-5070	morileeinc.com
Paloma Blanca		(416) 504-4550	palomablanca.com
Priscilla of Boston		(617) 242-2677	priscillaofboston.com
Private Label by G	(800) 858-3338	(562) 531-1116	privatelabelbyg.com
Pronovias	(888) 776-6684	(516) 371-0877	pronovias.com
St. Pucchi		(214) 631-8738	stpucchi.com
Sweetheart	(800) 223-6061	(212) 947-7171	gowns.com
Venus	(800) 648-3687	(626) 285-5796	lotusorient.com

Bridesmaid Manufacturers

Alyce Designs		(847) 966-9200	alycedesigns.com
Bari Jay		(212) 391-1555	bari-jay.com
Belsoie	(800) 634-0224	(630) 295-5880.	belsoie.com
Bill Levkoff	(800) LEV-KOFF	(212) 221-0085	billlevkoff.com
Champagne	(888) 524-2672	(212) 302-9162	champagneformals.com
Dessy Creations	(800) DESSY-11	(212) 354-5808	dessy.com
New Image	(800) 421-IMAGE	(212) 764-0477	newimagebridesmaids.com
Watters and Watters		(972) 960-9884	watters.com, wtoo.com

Dress discounters

Discount Bridal Service	discountbridlaservice.com
PearlsPlace	PearlsPlace.com
BrideSave.com	BrideSave.com
Gowns Online	gownsonline.com
NetBride	netbride.com
RK Bridal	rkbridal.com
Romantic Headlines	romanticheadlines.com
David's Bridal	davidsbridal.com

Favors

Keepsakes & Promises	weddingfavors.com
Per Favore	perfavore.com
Favorite Things.com	favorite-things.com
A Kiss Glass Sculptures	lymans.com/akiss

Flowers

2G Roses	freshroses.com
Flowersales.com	flowersales.com
International Floral Picture Database	floralbase.com

Invitations

Rexcraft	rexcraft.com
Catalog Orders	catalog.orders.com
Formal-Invitations	formal-invitations.com
Busy Bride	thebusybride.com
Wedding Links Galore	weddinglinksgalore.com
OurBeginning.com	OurBeginning.com

Major invitation printers

Name	Toll-free	Phone	Web site address
Carlson Craft	(800) 328-1782		carlsoncraft.com
Crane	(800) 472-7263		crane.com
Embossed Graphics	(800) 362-6773	(630) 236-4001	embossed.com
Encore	(800) 526-0497		encorestudios.com
Regency		(717) 762-7161	regencythermo.com
William Arthur	(800) 985-6581	(207) 985-6581	williamarthur.com

Single Use Cameras

The Ultimate Online Wedding Mall	
	http://stores.yahoo. com/ultimatewedding/discam.html
C & G Disposable cameras	cngdisposablecamera.com
Cameras Unlimited	blarg.net/~camsinc

Chapter 7: Community

About.com	About.com
UltimateWedding.com's Wedding Chat	ultimatewedding.com
Yahoo Clubs	http://clubs.yahoo.com
Delphi Wedding Forums	http://forums.delphi.com
Town & Country magazine	tncwedding.com
Hotmail	hotmail.com

Chapter 8: Advice

Crane's Online Wedding Blue Book	
	crane.com/wedding_blue_ book.html or crane.com
Etiquette Hell	thinds.com/jmh/ehell/index.htm

Chapter 9: Register

Della Weddings	Della.com
Ewish	ewish.com
WishClick	wishclick.com
The Gift.com	thegift.com
Williams-Sonoma	williams-sonoma.com
Michael Round	mround.com
Bridal Tips	BridalTips.com

Chapter 10: Grooms

Ungroom'd	ungroomed.com
Wedding Ring Hotline	weddingringhotline.com
Diamond Cutters	diamondcutters.com
Diamond Cutters International's	diamondcuttersintl.com
Diamond Grading	diamondgrading.com

Soc.Couples.Weddings FAQ on diamond buying
wam.umd.edu/~sek/wedding/ mlynek.html
5c Diamonds   5cdiamonds.com

Tuxes
Gingiss   gingiss.com
4Tuxedoes   4tuxedoes.com
eTuxedo   etuxedo.com

Chapter 11: Honeymoons
Best Fares' free "Newsdesk"   bestfares.com
Last Minute Travel   lastminutetravel.com
Priceline   Priceline.com
Travelocity.com   travelocity.com
Microsoft's Expedia   expedia.com
Lowest Fare   LowestFare.com
Bid4Travel   Bid4Travel.com
Budget Car rentals   DriveBudget.com
Hotel Reservations Network   180096hotel.com
QuickBook   QuickBook.com
1travel   onetravel.com
Sun Trips   suntrips.com
Apple Vacations   applevacations.com
Destination Weddings & Honeymoon magazine   dwhmagazine.com
Wedding Trips   weddingtrips.com

Appendix A: Power Net Tips
Elink   elinkmail.com

Index

Notes

Notes

BRIDAL BARGAINS

The Fields' first best-seller, over 400,000 copies sold!

"If you're getting married, you need this book!"
—Oprah Winfrey

WOW! Finally, a book on weddings you can actually use! With average U.S. wedding costs soaring near $20,000, you need creative and innovative solutions to planning a wonderful wedding on a realistic budget. *Bridal Bargains* is the answer! Inside you'll discover:

- ❖ HOW TO SAVE up to 40% on brand new, nationally advertised wedding dresses.
- ❖ THE BEST WEB SITES to save on everything from flowers to gowns, invitations to, well, you name it.
- ❖ 14 creative ways to CUT THE CATERING BILL at your reception.
- ❖ How to order FLOWERS AT WHOLESALE over the internet.
- ❖ ELEVEN QUESTIONS YOU SHOULD ASK ANY PHOTOGRAPHER—and seven money saving tips to lower that photo expense.
- ❖ How to do your INVITATIONS ON A COMPUTER, saving 70%.
- ❖ A CLEVER TRICK to save big bucks on your wedding cake.
- ❖ Plus many MONEY-SAVING TIPS ON WEDDING VIDEOS, RINGS, ENTERTAINMENT and more!

MONEY BACK GUARANTEE: If *Bridal Bargains* doesn't save you at least $500 on your wedding, then we will give you a complete refund. No kidding.

Just
$13.95
(Plus $3 shipping)

Call toll-free to order! 1-800-888-0385
or order online at www.windsorpeak.com
Mastercard, VISA, American Express and Discover Accepted!

Your New House

*The alert consumer's guide
to buying and building
a quality home.*

*"This is, by far, the best book available
on how to buy and build a new home!"*
—Robert Bruss,
Chicago Tribune

With the cost of buying a new home these days, you need more than just a little help. And we've got just the book for you: YOUR NEW HOUSE. Just like our other books, we give you page after page of helpful tips, including questions to ask, scams to avoid, and step-by-step strategies. Whether buying a new home is just over the horizon or a long-term goal, get a copy of YOUR NEW HOUSE today.

As featured on
ABC's 20/20 and
"Good Morning America"

Just
$14.95
(Plus $3 shipping)

*Call toll-free to order! 1-800-888-0385
or order online at www.windsorpeak.com*
Mastercard, VISA, American Express and Discover Accepted!

HOW TO REACH
THE AUTHORS

Have a question about

CyberBride?

Want to make
a suggestion?

Discovered a great tip
you'd like to share?

Contact the authors,
Denise & Alan Fields
in one of five ways:

1. By phone:
(303) 442-8792.

2. By mail:
436 Pine Street,
Boulder, CO 80302.

3. By fax:
(303) 442-3744.

4. By email:
questions@CyberBrideBook.com

5. On our web page:
http://www.CyberBrideBook.com

*(If this address isn't active, try our main web page at
www.WindsorPeak.com. Or call our office at 1-800-888-0385).*

Surf the CyberBride web site!

It's Murphy's Law of books—as soon as we go to press, something in this book changes. Pop onto our web site to check the latest updates on *CyberBride:*

www.CyberBrideBook.com

You'll read about:

❖ THE LATEST NEWS on tying the knot online.

❖ HINTS & TIPS from recent brides in our "mail bag."

❖ NEW SITES suggested by our readers.

❖ CORRECTIONS and clarifications.

❖ LINKS to our other great site, BridalGown.com.

Best of all, it's free!

If this site is not active, try our main site at
www.windsorpeak.com
or call our office at
1-800-888-0385 for the latest address!